CULTURES OF THE WORLD

KENYA

Robert Pateman

MARSHALL CAVENDISH
New York • London • Sydney

Reference Edition reprinted 1999 by
Marshall Cavendish Corporation
99 White Plains Road
Tarrytown
New York 10591

© Times Editions Pte Ltd 1996, 1993

Originated and designed by
Times Books International, an imprint of
Times Editions Pte Ltd

Printed in Malaysia

Library of Congress Cataloging-in-Publication Data:
Pateman, Robert
    Kenya / Robert Pateman.
      p. cm.—(Cultures Of The World)
    Includes bibliographical references and index.
    Summary: Describes the geography, history,
    government, economy, and culture of Kenya.
    ISBN 1-85435-572-4
    1. Kenya—Juvenile literature. [1. Kenya.]
    I. Title. II. Series.
DT433.522.P38 1993
967.62—dc20   92–39263
               CIP
               AC

INTRODUCTION

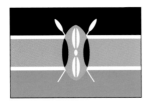

TO THE REST OF THE WORLD Kenya is best known for its wildlife, but Kenya is also a nation of many different tribes and cultures. At the turn of the century, the tribes that lived in the part of East Africa we now know as Kenya had no concept of being a nation. It was the European colonialists who drew up the boundaries of modern Kenya.

Yet, in only a short time, the idea of Kenyan nationhood has taken firm root, and Kenya is now considered one of the most successful countries in modern Africa. In recent years tribal tensions, drought, and a fast-growing population have threatened Kenya's economic and social progress. Despite this, there are good reasons to be optimistic about Kenya's future, as this book, part of the *Cultures of the World* series, will reveal.

CONTENTS

Samburu ("sahm-BOO-roo") warrior—the ivory earrings are traditionally worn only after the circumcision ceremony marking a boy's entrance to manhood.

CONTENTS

Stone sculpting is now extremely popular in Kenya, especially because of the recent explosion in tourism.

5

GEOGRAPHY

KENYA IS SITUATED on the east coast of Africa. It shares land borders with five countries: Tanzania to the south, Uganda to the west, Sudan and Ethiopia to the north, and Somalia to the east. It also has an eastern coastline that is bounded by the Indian Ocean. The equator runs through the center of the country.

Covering 224,960 square miles (582,646 square kilometers), Kenya is about the same size as Texas, or slightly larger than France. It is divided into four main geographical regions: a coastal plain, an interior area of bush and grassland, the fertile highlands, and a dry northern plateau.

With much of northern Kenya being semi-arid desert, 85% of the population is crowded into the fertile southern two-thirds of the country. In less than a century, the capital, Nairobi, has grown from a small railway junction into a city of over 1.2 million people. However, the vast majority of Kenya's population are still farmers.

Opposite: **Flowers in the Aberdare National Park.**

Left: **A sign to mark the position of the equator.**

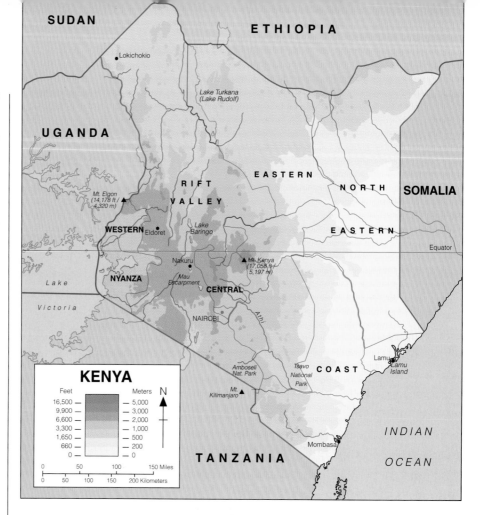

Kenya's climate varies according to altitude and rainfall. The equator runs through Kenya and the area to the north is extremely dry. In contrast, Mt. Kenya is capped with snow year round and has several glaciers on the slopes.

KENYA

Feet		Meters
16,500 —		— 5,000
9,900 —		— 3,000
6,600 —		— 2,000
3,300 —		— 1,000
1,650 —		— 500
660 —		— 200
0 —		— 0

N

0   50   100   150 Miles
0   50   100   150   200 Kilometers

CLIMATE AND SEASONS

Because the equator runs through Kenya, it does not have the four seasons that many countries enjoy. Instead of a change in temperature, the most noticeable change in the weather pattern is marked by rainfall. Kenya has two rainy seasons. In a typical year, the "long" rains arrive in April and last until June. The "short" rains generally start in October and may last until December. But this pattern can vary in different regions.

The short rains usually fall more in the mornings, followed by long periods of afternoon sunshine. The long rains bring heavier, more regular, and longer-lasting rainstorms. The two rainy seasons last for approximately three months each but far more rain falls during the long rains.

January and February, and then August through September, are very dry months. During these times, many rivers and lakes dry up completely.

The rainy season affects the coastal, central, and western parts of the country. These regions receive around 40 inches (100 centimeters) of rain a year. The wettest areas are on the coastal belt and the land west of Lake Victoria.

The area north of the equator is extremely dry. For a short period of time in April the area receives rain, but these rains are unpredictable. Water may be obtained from rivers, but for much of the year, these rivers are only dry, sandy beds.

Temperatures in Kenya vary more with altitude than with the time of year. Along the coast, the temperatures average 80°F (27°C). In contrast, Nairobi lies at an altitude of 5,500 feet (1,676 meters) and has far cooler temperatures. Indeed, evenings in the capital can be quite cold, and people need to wear warmer clothing.

Northeastern Kenya is extremely dry and arid, and is a harsh, demanding environment for both humans and beasts.

A panoramic view of the Great Rift Valley from Losiolo in northern Kenya.

THE GREAT RIFT VALLEY

The Great Rift Valley is one of the most remarkable natural features on the planet. It is a 4,000 mile (6,440 kilometer) long fissure in the earth's crust that starts in the Middle East and stretches to Mozambique. In East Africa, it breaks into two branches, one of which passes through Kenya. The rift was formed in prehistoric times when the land shifted to create a valley.

The course of the Rift Valley becomes quite clear if seen from outer space, because it is marked by a series of lakes. However, on the ground, it is not always so obvious. At Lake Turkana in northern Kenya, it is almost impossible to tell that one is standing in a valley. Farther south, cliffs 2,000 or 3,000 feet (600 or 900 meters) high drop dramatically to the valley floor. The valley and its lakes form an important refuge for wildlife.

MOUNTAINS

Much of Kenya is mountainous. Within the Kenyan Highlands are two major mountain ranges running north to south on either side of the Great Rift Valley. To the west lies the Mau Escarpment and to the east the Aberdares.

Mount Kenya is located east of the highlands. At 17,058 feet (5,197 meters), it is the highest mountain in the country and the second highest in Africa. It is an extinct volcano with twin peaks. There are several glaciers on the slopes, and the top is covered with snow throughout the year. The mountain sits virtually on the equator and forms a dramatic border between Kenya's highland and lowland.

The higher slopes of Mount Kenya receive very heavy rainfall. The vegetation here is different from anywhere else in the country. In fact, 13 plants growing on Mount Kenya are found nowhere else in the world. The rain that flows down the slopes makes the area below some of the most fertile farmland in the country.

Kenya's second highest mountain is Mount Elgon. It is located much farther west on the Kenyan-Ugandan border. At 14,178 feet (4,320 meters), it is high enough to sometimes have snow on the summit.

The twin peaks of Mount Kenya, called Batian and Nelion.

Modern high-rise office buildings in Nairobi.

NAIROBI

Nairobi is one of the most beautiful and modern cities in Africa. It is the home of the country's parliament, the main commercial center, and the hub of Kenya's communication system. The city has many modern facilities, including a major international airport, a world-class museum, and a good university. The Kenyatta Conference Center is perhaps the most famous landmark. Many important trade fairs and conferences are staged here. There are also Olympic-standard sports facilities that were built for the 1987 All African Games.

Nairobi has a pleasant climate because of its high elevation, and is free of the malaria that plagues the coastal regions. It is a cosmopolitan city and has an influential European and Indian population. Its population is over 1.2 million, and it is one of the fastest growing cities in the world.

Close to the city is the Nairobi National Park, where it is possible to photograph wildlife with the city skyline in the background.

It is sometimes forgotten that Nairobi is not yet a hundred years old. It was founded in 1899, when the railway that was being built from the coast reached this point. The area was known as "Nyrobi," or "the place of cool waters," by the few Masai ("mah-SAI") who grazed their cattle in the region. As the last flat ground before the steep Great Rift Valley escarpment, it was chosen as the site for a base camp. Almost overnight, an enormous tent camp grew up to house thousands of railway workers. A permanent settlement was never planned here.

The influx of people from the rural areas has led to serious social problems in Nairobi, and poverty has caused many to turn to crime.

However, Nairobi became the natural town to serve the needs of the white farmers who slowly settled along the railway line. During the colonial period, Nairobi became the most important town in all of British East Africa.

Despite its modern appearance, Nairobi faces many problems today. With so many people moving in from the countryside, shanty towns such as Mathare Valley have grown up around the city edges. Here, people live in crowded homes built out of discarded scrap materials. There is little or no running water or electricity, and the living conditions are miserable and unhealthy.

The growth of these slum areas has led to a serious crime wave. People in the rich neighborhoods have high walls surrounding their houses, and employ guards to protect them.

OTHER CITIES

Mombasa ("mohm-BAH-sah") is Kenya's second major city and is about two thirds the size of Nairobi with a population of 800,000. It is built on an island and has a much longer history than the capital. The first Arab traders founded Mombasa in the 11th century. The old part of the city consists of narrow winding streets and Arab-style houses. For a short time at the end of the 16th century, the city was controlled by the Portuguese, who built Fort Jesus to guard the entrance to the old harbor. The fort is well preserved, and is one of Kenya's most important historic buildings.

Mombasa's harbor, Kilindini ("kil-in-DEE-nee"), dominates the commercial life of the city. Established here because there is a safe channel through the coral reef for ships to sail into the harbor, Kilindini is a trading center and a major resting point for naval ships. The large harbor has enabled Mombasa to become the site of Kenya's oil refining industry. Many factories have also been built to take advantage of the harbor facilities.

Mombasa, Kenya's main port, is an important industrial center as well as a major resting point for shipping in the Indian Ocean.

Kenya is still very much an agricultural society. Most of Kenya's other towns and cities grew up to serve the surrounding agricultural regions. Kisumu ("ki-SOO-moo"), on Lake Victoria, operates as the main harbor on the lake. Although political problems have drastically cut the amount of goods being ferried between Kenya and Tanzania, it remains an important business center for this heavily populated region.

Nakuru ("na-KOO-roo") is the most important town in the Kenyan Highlands, but it is relatively small, with a population of just over 100,000. The only other towns with a population of more than 50,000 are Eldoret ("EL-door-et"), Machakos ("mah-CHAH-kos"), and Meru ("MAY-ru"). Lamu Town, the center of the country's Muslim community, dates back to the time of the original Arab incursions into East Africa.

A *jahazi* (sailing boat) in front of Fort Omani, Lamu Town. Lamu, an island off the northern coast of Kenya, is the center of the country's small Muslim community.

FLORA

Since Kenya has so many different regions, it is home to a marvelous range of flowers, shrubs, and trees. After the rains, even the desert bursts into flower. A good example of the variety of Kenyan plant life is seen on the slopes of Mount Elgon, where the forest contains 62 different species of

The famous baobab tree, capable of storing much water in its spongy trunk for the dry seasons.

trees. In contrast, it would be very unusual to find a forest in North America or Europe that had more than 25 different species. Sadly, many of Kenya's native trees, such as the baobab ("BAY-oh-bab"), or the fig, take a long time to grow. If they are cut for commercial purposes, they are often replaced with faster growing trees from Australia or South America.

Each region in Kenya has a unique flora. Along the coast, palms and mangroves are the most typical plants. The dry plains and northern areas are dominated by low bush, scrub, and grassland. The highlands were originally covered in forest, much of which has now been cleared. African camphor, African olive, and pencil cedar are typical trees of this region.

The baobab is probably Kenya's most famous tree. It is found in many different parts of the country and can grow in the drier areas if there is underground water. It has a strange upside-down appearance that makes it seem as though its roots are sticking into the air and its trunk into the ground. Its hollowed-out trunk is used to make canoes or water holders, the bark fibers can be twisted into ropes and baskets, the leaves and fruit pulp are made into medicine, and the seeds and leaves are edible.

ENDANGERED WILDLIFE

Kenya has put aside large areas of land for the preservation of wildlife. It has also banned all hunting in the country, despite the fact that hunting safaris are very profitable. Unfortunately, the future of many species is by no means safe.

Many of the parks suffer from poaching, often by organized and well-armed gangs. The very size of the park system makes it impossible to effectively patrol the whole area. Although much of the poaching is known to be the work of raiders from across the border, Kenyans are also involved.

Poaching and drought have already decimated the country's rhinoceros population to a point where it is unlikely to ever recover. The elephant herds have also suffered badly over the last 10 years. However, early reports suggest that a worldwide ban on ivory has slowed the rate of poaching.

Even if poaching can be controlled, the conflict between wildlife and Kenya's growing population will almost certainly become worse in the near future. At present, the government is anxious to preserve the parks for the profitable tourist industry, but many farmers see the animals as a nuisance or even a danger. It is difficult for them to understand why they cannot graze their cattle or grow crops in a national park when their own land has become badly overcrowded.

FAUNA

Kenya is famous for its magnificent wildlife, which is abundant and varied. The country has developed an extensive network of game parks to help protect this precious heritage.

By far the most numerous groups, in both number and species, are the insects and arachnids. There are 600 species of butterflies alone. Perhaps the most dramatic of the insects are the termites, some species of which build great towering nests above the plains. These nests are made from earth, cemented together with the termites' droppings and saliva until they are as hard as bricks.

Many lizards, birds, and frogs feed on the insects, and these in turn provide the main source of food for small carnivores such as mongooses, birds of prey, and snakes. There are as many as 100 species of snake in Kenya, several of which are poisonous. But they are not particularly dangerous to humans, as most snakes are shy and will move away when they sense people approaching.

The largest of the reptiles in Kenya is the Nile crocodile. Sadly, it has suffered from hunting and poaching. Lizards range from giant monitor lizards that can grow to six feet (1.8 meters) long, to tiny geckos found in most homes. Adhesive pads on the geckos' toes allow them to run up walls or even hang upside down from the ceiling. The larger mammals include elephants, giraffes, zebras, rhinoceroses, and many different types of antelope.

A cheetah sits with two adult cubs on a termite mound. Kenya teems with an enormous variety of wildlife in its many game parks.

An acacia tree with the nests of many weaver birds hanging from its branches.

Many animals in Kenya can live together in the same area because they have different eating habits. Zebras, for example, graze on the tops of the grass, while gazelles prefer leaves and shoots that grow close to the ground.

Some of the larger antelopes tend to be browsers and take their food from trees and bushes. Elephants and giraffes can find food in the highest trees no other animal can reach.

Predators such as lions, cheetahs, and wild dogs will hunt and kill the large animals. Usually they will only take the slowest and weakest animals, and so do not affect the balance of wildlife. After the predators have made a kill, scavenging animals swoop in to claim part of the food. The vultures will often be the first to arrive, quickly followed by the jackals.

Kenya's wildlife varies from region to region. In the dry areas of the north, the reticulated giraffe and the Grevy's zebra have quite different markings from similar animals found elsewhere in the country. The bongo (a kind of antelope), the giant forest hog, and the beautiful black and white colobus monkey are found in the mountainous areas.

THE GAME PARKS

Kenya has established an extensive network of game parks and reserves to protect its wildlife. Some of the most important parks include:

ABERDARE NATIONAL PARK

Located in the central highlands, the park has two famous lodges—"Treetops" and "The Ark." This is one of the few places to see the bongo. The thick forest cover has allowed a few rhinoceroses to escape poachers.

AMBOSELI NATIONAL PARK

A semi-arid area found in the south, it is noted for spectacular views of Mount Kilimanjaro, which lies just across the border in Tanzania. Most of Kenya's large mammals are found here. It is one of the best places to see the elusive cheetah.

LAKE NAKURU NATIONAL PARK

The park consists of the lake and surrounding areas of swamp and bush. It is famous for its bird life. If the conditions are right, thousands of flamingos will gather on the lake.

MASAI MARA NATIONAL RESERVE

A large park with extensive areas of open grassland, it borders Tanzania's Serengeti National Park and is an important dry-season refuge for many animals. During the July-October dry season, over a million wildebeest usually move into the Mara. The park has Kenya's largest population of lions.

MERU NATIONAL PARK

This area of thorny bush land located northeast of Mount Kenya has rare animals including the reticulated giraffe, gerenuk, and Somalian ostrich. This park, where Joy and George Adamson returned lions and cheetahs to the wild, is featured in the movie *Born Free*.

MOUNT ELGON NATIONAL PARK

The park is situated on the slopes of Kenya's second highest mountain. Vegetation ranges from bamboo forests to swampland. Elgon is famous for its elephants. These elephants have learned to go deep into caves in their search for salt.

NAIROBI NATIONAL PARK

This park is a very important dry-season refuge for the large number of animals that usually live on the plains to the south. Human habitation along the Athi River is now making it more difficult for wildlife to move north into the park. Most of Kenya's large mammals can be found here, although there are no elephants.

SAIWA SWAMP NATIONAL PARK

Situated in western Kenya, Saiwa is the country's smallest game park. It was established on a tiny area of swamp to protect a small population of rare Sitatunga antelope.

SAMBURU NATIONAL PARK

Situated north of Mount Kenya, this is a wood-land and bush park on the edge of the desert. Unusual animals include the gerenuk, reticulated giraffe, and Grevy's zebra.

SIBILOI NATIONAL PARK

Situated on the east side of Lake Turkana, the park is an important refuge for the world's largest population of crocodiles. Other animals include the lion, cheetah, and oryx.

TSAVO NATIONAL PARK

An enormous park that consists mainly of bush with some wooded areas, it is home to large populations of zebra, buffalo, antelope, and lion. The size of the park makes it difficult for rangers to patrol, and poachers have taken a heavy toll on the animal populations.

HISTORY

KENYA, AS A NATION, IS A MODERN CONCEPT. Its borders are the invention of the Europeans, and the early history of the land can only be told as part of the history of East Africa.

The Africans themselves have left no written records of their history. We can learn something from archeological digs, as well as from studying the language, culture, and traditional stories of the tribes.

However, there are still considerable gaps in our knowledge. Very little was known about the interior of the country before the 19th century, and this little was based on legends of doubtful authenticity. Early Kenyan history is shrouded in mystery.

Opposite: **The magnificent fiberglass tusks that span Moi Avenue in Mombasa.**

Left: **The ruins of an ancient Arab palace near the coast. Arab traders were the first outsiders to enter Kenya.**

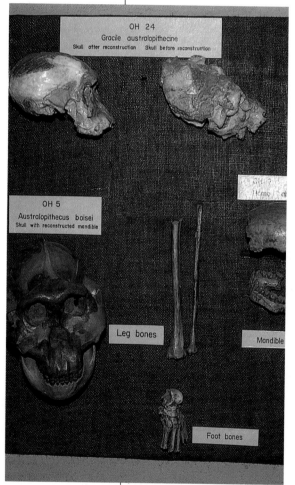

OH 24
Gracile australopithecine
Skull after reconstruction   Skull before reconstruction

OH 5
Australopithecus boisei
Skull with reconstructed mandible

Leg bones

Mandible

Foot bones

Some of the oldest human remains in the world are displayed in the National Museum, Nairobi.

AFRICA—THE BIRTHPLACE OF HUMANITY

The oldest fossil records of humans and their ancestors have come from archeological digs in Tanzania, Ethiopia, and Lake Turkana in northern Kenya.

In the early 1960s, Louis Leakey and his wife, Mary, discovered fragments of teeth and a jawbone from a human-like creature they estimated to be 14 million years old. This was the earliest evidence of human evolution ever discovered. Their son, Richard Leakey, has continued their work, finding complete human skulls that are 3 million years old. The discoveries made by the Leakey family strongly suggest that East Africa was the birthplace of humanity. We certainly know that people using stone tools were living in the Rift Valley around 40,000 years ago, for their ax tools and cave drawings are still being discovered.

However, the next part of African history is clouded in mystery. We know virtually nothing about the hunting and gathering people who eventually came to settle in the region, although it is thought they might be similar to the bushmen who still live in southern Africa.

Tribes who have retained a hunting and gathering lifestyle, such as the Boni ("BO-ni") and Wata, may be ancestors of these early inhabitants.

INVASION

About 2,000 years ago, East Africa started to receive a massive influx of new people. Although consisting of many different tribes, they shared a similar language and are identified as Bantu ("BAN-too") speaking peoples. They drifted from the west, across Africa, eventually mixing with the societies that already occupied Kenya.

These Bantu people prospered and their influence spread because they farmed the land, which allowed them to support a much larger population. They also brought with them the knowledge of making iron. As a result there are many tribes, including the Kikuyu ("ki-KOO-yoo"), which are regarded as Bantu people and they make up the majority of Kenya's population. The migration reached its peak in the 14th and 15th centuries, and changed the face of Africa, but we know little about this event.

During this time other migrations were taking place. The Nilotic ("ni-LOT-ik") and Cushitic ("koo-SHIT-ik") tribes started to move in from the north and northeast. The Nilotic tribes include the Masai and the Samburu who still maintain many of the traditional ways of their migratory ancestors. It was due to these migrations that Kenya today is a nation of so many different tribes and cultures.

A *moran* ("MAHR-en") of the Samburu tribe. The Samburu came to Kenya as part of the Nilotic migration from the north.

OUTSIDERS ARRIVE

Between the 7th and 10th centuries, the Kenyan coast was settled by Arab traders. Often fleeing wars in their homeland, the Arabs built forts and cities and established trade with the interior of the country. Despite continually fighting among themselves, these Arab communities grew rich and powerful.

During the 15th century, Portuguese explorers started to sail their tiny ships along the coast of Africa. In 1498, Vasco da Gama finally succeeded in rounding the Cape of Good Hope, and soon Portuguese fleets were exploring the east coast of the continent. They were amazed to find

Seats where Arab traders would have waited for the arrival of their ships.

wealthy Arab settlements where they had expected a wilderness. The Portuguese soon established their own trading centers and, for the next two centuries, they fought with the Arabs for control of the East African coastline. The most lasting reminder of Portuguese influence is Fort Jesus in Mombasa. Built in 1593, it still stands today. After many sieges, the fort was finally captured by the Arabs in 1698, bringing Portuguese influence in the region to an end.

As Portugal's fortunes declined, other European powers such as Britain, France, and Germany began to take an interest in East Africa. European missionaries, often given assistance by Arab rulers on the coast, explored the interior of the continent. In 1849, Johann Krapf and Johannes Rebmann became the first Europeans to see Mount Kenya. Three years later, John Speke was the first white man to reach Lake Victoria, where he discovered the major source of the Nile.

THE GREAT SIEGE

The Portuguese never had a large army in Africa, and most of their supplies had to be brought in by ship from their colonies in India. The great Mombasa fortress suffered many sieges, including one from the Wasimba ("wah-SIM-bah") tribe—fierce African warriors who became unlikely allies of the Arabs. The final and greatest siege started in March 1696, when the fortress and town were bombarded by an Arab fleet. There were only 50 Portuguese in the fort with several hundred local people. From the beginning, food was short and the defenders had to make daring raids at night to bring in supplies.

On Christmas Day, four Portuguese ships sailed into the bay and the fortress was believed to be saved. However, the fleet came under attack and had to flee, leaving the desperate defenders to their fate. Next, bubonic plague broke out, sparing only a handful of people. However, the Arabs did not attempt to storm the walls, and, in September, a fleet was able to bring in a large force of Portuguese and Indian troops to relieve the defenders.

Still the siege continued until, two years and nine months after it started, Arab soldiers finally scaled the walls. They found only a dozen survivors, whom they immediately executed. One story tells how a young boy promised to show the attackers a store of gold, only to lead them into the gunpowder storeroom that he then blew up, killing himself and all those around him.

DIVIDING UP AFRICA

Although trade, missionary work, and exploration took place, the European powers had little political control over Africa until the 1880s. In 1884, there was a conference in Berlin where it was decided to which areas of Africa each European nation would have first claim. The purpose of the conference was to prevent arguments and possible armed conflict between the European powers. However, the result was a scramble, as each nation raced to colonize its part of the continent.

It was agreed in Berlin that all the lands north of the middle of Lake Victoria would come under the British sphere of influence. This included not only modern Kenya, but also Uganda. This area was of particular concern to the British because they had a considerable investment in Egypt, and consequently were anxious to control the source of the River Nile.

The Imperial British East African Company was established to develop this new interest, but it soon ran into financial troubles. The British had to step in and take over the management of the area. Despite this, they had little interest in Kenya, where the Masai and Nandi ("NAHN-dee") tribes were fierce warriors, but Uganda was seen by Britain as a land of great potential.

Britain
Germany
Belgium
Portugal
Spain
France
Italy
Independent

KENYA

By the late 19th century, the European powers had carved the continent of Africa into areas of influence.

THE RAILWAY

In 1896, Britain started to build a railway to link Uganda with the coast. By 1899, the line had reached the site of modern-day Nairobi, and a large town quickly grew up there. Having built the railway, the British needed somebody to use it, so white farmers were encouraged to come to Kenya and settle along the railway line. In 1900, there were an estimated 480 Europeans living in Kenya. By 1915, this number had grown to 5,000, and they had taken over large areas of land.

Reserves, usually on inferior land, were set up for the displaced Africans, who came mainly from the Kipsigis ("KIP-si-gis"), Masai, and Nandi tribes. The Africans, with no central government, could offer little opposition to the British and their modern weapons. When, in 1905, the Nandi finally started to resist the British, they suffered brutal reprisals in which thousands were killed.

The years 1900 to 1914 were a period of increasing European influence in Africa. At the same time, the work of the missionaries brought Christianity and education to many Africans.

The railway was vital in the shaping of present-day Kenya. It is because of this important transportation link that the interior of the country and agriculture were able to flourish.

29

POLITICAL CHANGES

After World War I, Britain somewhat reluctantly took over the government of the former German area of Tanganyika (now Tanzania). This left them with an enormous East African empire. After the war, many soldiers seeking a better life emigrated to Kenya. In 1920, the country changed from a protectorate to a colony. Much of the highlands were reserved for white settlement. Africans were only allowed in the area if they worked there, and identity cards were issued. Taxes were also imposed on the Africans, in an attempt to force them into working on the plantations.

The war had changed the Africans' view of the Europeans. They had seen white men killing white men, and found that this contradicted the message of the missionaries. At the same time, more Kenyans were emerging from the missionary schools with an education. The result was the birth of the independence movement. During the 1920s, the Kikuyu tribe formed their first political parties.

AN AFRICAN HERO

In 1922, a young African leader named Harry Thuku was arrested for political activity. Thousands of people gathered in Nairobi to protest his detention. Although noisy, the protesters did not seem violent or threatening. However, the police became nervous about the large crowd and opened fire. In the confusion that followed, an unknown number of people were killed—reports ranged from 20 to over 100, with many more injured. This shattering event marked the real start of the Kenyan independence struggle.

UPRISING

Shortly after World War II, two Africans were appointed to the Legislative Council that governed Kenya. This was progress, but certainly not a fair representation or anywhere near enough to satisfy the growing demands of the Kenyans. In 1946, a new party was formed called the Kenya African Union, and Jomo Kenyatta returned from England to take over its leadership. The KAU was a predominantly Kikuyu organization. The party became involved in strikes and unrest that often threatened law and order.

In 1951, with their power growing, the KAU issued a five-point document of demands. When these were rejected, the stage was set for more violent protests. The following year, African freedom fighters started to slaughter European-owned cattle and murder Africans believed to support the white rulers. These resistance fighters became known as the Mau Mau. As a result, the white rulers declared a state of emergency. Jomo Kenyatta and other political leaders were arrested and imprisoned.

By 1953, the Europeans themselves became the target of attacks. Over the next three years, 32 white settlers were killed. In the same period, thousands of Kenyans, suspected of being part of the Mau Mau movement, died at the hands of government soldiers. The British were able to defeat the uprising with military force, but world opinion had turned against them. Other African countries were being given their independence, and it was now inevitable that Kenya would also gain self-rule.

President Kenyatta, the founding father of modern Kenya, was a charismatic leader who forged Kenya into a unified and stable nation.

INDEPENDENCE AND AFTER

In 1960, at the first election prior to full independence, two powerful parties emerged—the KANU (Kenya African National Union) and the KADU (Kenya African Democratic Union).

Later in the year, Kenyatta was finally released from prison. He immediately became the symbol of freedom to all tribes, and both parties sought his support. He eventually agreed to lead the KANU party. With Kenyatta's support, KANU won a commanding victory in the 1963 elections. On December 12, 1963, Kenya became an independent country.

In 1978, President Kenyatta died. Fortunately, there was a peaceful transfer of power, and Vice President Daniel arap Moi became the second

The new Kenyatta Conference Center—a monument to Kenya's recent progress.

AN EXCITING BUT UNCERTAIN FUTURE

At the end of 1991, the Kenyan government bowed to international pressure and agreed to allow a more democratic form of government. Several new political parties formed and managed to win nearly half the seats in the National Assembly in the December 1992 elections. These first steps toward democracy were marred by serious outbreaks of tribal violence in the west of the country, with reports of hundreds of people being killed and many more injured. Less than a month after the elections President Moi suspended parliament, saying it was too unruly. There were also reported arrests and detention of newspaper and television journalists who opposed the government.

President Moi was re-elected with only 37% of the popular vote but his opposition is divided into very small groups which are unable to unite against him. The Assembly passed a law that a president can serve no more than two terms but the law was not made retrospective, which means that Moi will be eligible to stand for re-election in 1997.

In the background of this volatile political situation are other complicating factors: Kenya suffers from a population that is growing faster than its economy; the presence of thousands of refugees fleeing unrest in neighbouring Sudan, Ethiopia, and Somalia; and recurring droughts that have hampered Kenya's ability to profit from agriculture.

Maintaining political stability in Kenya without resorting to harsh and repressive tactics is the greatest challenge facing President Moi. If tribal differences can be overcome to form cohesive coalitions in the National Assembly a more stable political arena may emerge. Whether Kenya's fledgling democracy can survive the difficulties remains to be seen.

In foreign policy Kenya has maintained good relations with the West since independence. Its major trading partners are the United States and the European Union, with Britain its largest export market.

Kenyan president. However, in 1982, stability was unexpectedly shattered by a coup attempt led by some air force officers and several days of rioting and looting followed before order was restored.

Since then, Kenya has suffered regular periods of unrest and tensions between different tribal groups. In some cases drought and overpopulation have aggravated these tensions. The government, in its attempts to maintain order, has sometimes severely restricted people's freedom and has been criticized many times for human rights violations.

GOVERNMENT

KENYA IS A REPUBLIC with a president as the head of the government. It has close links with the West and is a member of the United Nations, the Organization for African Unity, and the Commonwealth of Nations.

FROM ONE PARTY TO MANY

The original Kenyan constitution had two legislative houses, like the United States. In 1967 these were merged into one parliament known as the National Assembly. In that year President Kenyatta also banned all but his own party, the KANU, from participation in national political life.

Bowing to international and domestic pressure, the government amended the constitution to allow for multiple parties in 1991 and in the 1992 elections other political parties were allowed to field candidates. The KANU party holds a majority of seats in the assembly.

Opposite: **Outside the Kenyatta Conference Center in Nairobi.**

Left: **Kenyatta Avenue, the hub of Kenya's political and social life.**

The Nairobi Parliament building.

THE NATIONAL ASSEMBLY

Every five years, elections are held for the positions of president and members of the National Assembly. Up until the last election, in 1992, anybody seeking office had to be a member of the KANU Party. Now several smaller parties hold seats in the assembly but even combined they are still a minority.

Every Kenyan over 18 is entitled to vote. The size of the National Assembly was increased in 1986, and today there are 188 elected seats. In addition, there are 12 seats that are filled by presidential appointment. The president often uses these seats to increase the number of women in the assembly. Two parliamentary positions, those of attorney general and assembly speaker, do not have voting powers.

After the election, the president hand-picks the cabinet and nominates the vice president. The cabinet is usually about 20-strong, with each cabinet member heading a department of the government.

Officially, the assembly controls expenditures and approves the government's budget. However, in practice, the assembly often does little more than debate and approve the president's wishes. Certainly anybody who openly opposes the president is unlikely to have much of a political future.

LOCAL POLITICS

Kenya is divided into seven provinces, plus the urban area of Nairobi. These are further subdivided into 40 districts. Below this level of government come divisions, locations, and sublocations. The provincial and district commissioners are appointed and answer to the president. They are responsible for areas such as education, health, and transportation, and they work alongside elected councils.

Heads of locations take the title of "chief." They are powerful figures responsible for raising funds for health, transportation, and self-help projects. They also mediate disputes and supervise law and order.

The chiefs and subchiefs have considerable day-to-day contact with the people in their area. The chiefs are expected to hold weekly open meetings, where new laws and policies are explained and local issues discussed. These meetings are usually well attended. They are seen as true democracy in action because they allow everybody a chance to have a say in government.

Opposite: **Jomo Kenyatta opening one of the Safari Rallies at the Conference Center in Nairobi.**

TWO PRESIDENTS

JOMO KENYATTA The first president of Kenya, he was born in Ngenda ("n-GEN-dah") sometime in the late 1890s. He attended missionary school from 1909 until 1914, where he was baptized Johnstone Kamu. He later worked for the Nairobi municipality and, after becoming involved in Kikuyu political groups, changed his name to Jomo Kenyatta.

By 1928, he had become secretary of the Kikuyu Central Association. The following year, he went to London to represent that organization. It was during his time in England that Kenyatta wrote his famous book, *Facing Mount Kenya*. He made numerous speeches, and pressured the British Parliament to grant Kenyans more say in running their own country. His work in England made Kenyatta famous back in his homeland, and he became a symbol of the Kenyan independence struggle.

When Kenyatta returned to Kenya in 1946, he became president of the newly formed Kenya African Union. In the 1950s, the colonial authorities suspected him of being involved with the Mau Mau uprising and imprisoned him. He was released in 1961 and helped KANU to victory in the 1963 election.

In 1963, Kenyatta became prime minister of an independent Kenya. Soon after achieving independence, Kenya became a republic and Kenyatta took the title of president. He was affectionately known as *Mzee* ("m-ZAY"), which can be translated as old one or wise one.

Throughout his rule, Kenyatta proved to be a conservative and tolerant leader, and Kenya became a moderate, stable, and pro-Western state. However, his greatest fear was that tribal tensions would destroy the new country, and he used this as justification for ruthlessly destroying any political opposition.

On August 22, 1978, Kenyatta died peacefully in his sleep.

DANIEL ARAP MOI President Moi was born in Baringo district in 1924. He is a member of the Kalenjin ("kal-en-JIN") tribe. He obtained his education at an African missionary school and, from 1945 to 1957, worked as a school teacher. At the same time he was also involved in politics. Between 1948 and 1954, he served on the country's legislative council. Moi joined the cabinet in 1961 as minister of education. He went on to become minister of home affairs and, in 1966, was elected vice president.

On the death of Kenyatta, Moi became president, and his position was confirmed in the election that followed. He has proved a strong and confident president but has increasingly been criticised for his forceful quashing of dissent.

Moi has also been an influential figure in African politics. In 1981 and 1982, he was chairman of the Organization of African Unity. Recently, Kenya was one of the first African nations to accept a visit from representatives of the South African government, and Moi again looks likely to set an example for other African leaders to follow. In 1992, he was elected to a fourth term in office.

THE ARMED FORCES

Kenya's relationships with Tanzania and Uganda have often been tense, and there is a long-standing land dispute with Somalia. As a result, Kenya maintains a strong military force. The army consists of 20,500 men and has around 80 tanks at its disposal. The air force (2,500 men) has a squadron of modern combat aircraft and a heavy force of helicopters. The navy (1,400 men), which is based in Mombasa, keeps a fleet of patrol boats and two modern guided-missile attack craft to guard the Kenyan coast.

Opposite: **Daniel Moi.**

Below: **A statue of Jomo Kenyatta at the Kenyatta Conference Center in Nairobi.**

THE FEAR OF TRIBAL TENSION

One reason the European colonial powers gave for not granting Kenya its independence was that the country's numerous tribes and ethnic groups would never be able to form a unified government.

The colonialists claimed that it was only their presence that kept Kenya from being ripped apart by tribal warfare. This has proved to be mainly false. In the more than 30 years since independence, Kenya has been one of Africa's most stable nations.

However, even Kenyan politicians acknowledge that ethnic differences could still pose a danger. Kenyatta himself traveled to villages and hamlets preaching his message of *harambee.* Attempting to unite the country, he included influential people from other ethnic groups in his government. Oginga Odinga from the Luo tribe was made vice president, and Tom Mboya, also a Luo, was given a cabinet position.

Nairobi today is a thriving, bustling city—a product of Kenya's political and economic stability.

Tom Mboya was murdered on July 5, 1969 and his mysterious death led to fighting between the Luo and Kikuyu communities. Oginda Odinga was affiliated with the Forum for the Restoration of Democracy (FORD), the biggest organized political opposition group in Kenya, until his death in 1994.

Many people now feel that it was only Kenyatta's personality that kept Kenya together and although the transfer of power to Daniel Moi proved to be peaceful, by 1992 clashes between tribes and the fear of racial violence had begun to affect the tourist trade and also interfere with crop production.

Alliances among tribal groups often take place along party political lines and the Kikuyus, among the most numerous of the groups in Kenya, feel that the government, in which they are not well represented, discriminates against them.

THE LEGAL SYSTEM

Before the establishment of a national government, disputes within the community were usually settled at a gathering of elders. In many tribes, only men could participate in the decision making. Cases might be discussed for weeks, or even years, before a majority was in agreement. Rulings of the elders were usually obeyed. To challenge their decision would bring the people involved into open conflict with the whole community.

If, for example, somebody caused the accidental death of another person, it was often the custom for him or her to pay a fine to the dead person's family. All the members of the defendant's family might contribute. Often, it was over a very long period of time that the fine was paid and the dispute settled.

Today, Kenya has a modern legal system. The Court of Appeal is the highest court in the land. It has jurisdiction over both criminal and civil laws, and rules on constitutional matters. This court is headed by the Chief Justice, who is one of seven Judges of Appeal.

Below the Court of Appeal is the High Court of Kenya. This court has jurisdiction over both criminal and civic laws, and receives appeals from lower courts.

Resident Magistrate Courts deal with lesser cases and have the power to imprison transgressors for up to five years or impose limited fines. District Magistrate Courts have jurisdiction over only minor offenses within their own area or district.

The Kenyan judicial system acknowledges the validity of traditional African customs in marriage, divorce, and matters affecting the family. For Muslims, there is also a Kadhi court that can be consulted on matters of Islamic law.

Although only a single judiciary is recognized in the Kenyan courts, Islamic customary law is also widely accepted.

ECONOMY

BY AFRICAN STANDARDS, Kenya is considered a successful country. Services such as banking and transportation are good, and political stability has encouraged Western nations to invest there. However, there are many problems and, compared with the West, Kenya is still a very poor nation. The average income is around $350 a year, and the standards of health care and education are not as high as in the developed world.

SUBSISTENCE FARMING

The Kenyan economy is centered on agriculture. Much of the land is still divided into small plots that support a single family. The family produces just enough food for its own needs, plus perhaps a little to sell in the local market. This is called subsistence farming.

The main crops grown in this way are corn, millet, sweet potatoes, cassava, potatoes, and fruits such as pineapples, coconuts, and bananas. Of these, corn is the most important and the staple diet of many Kenyans.

A typical farmer owns about one to three acres. His land may even be "fragmented," consisting of several tiny and separate plots. Often, he will be able to afford only the most basic tools, and most of the work will have to be done by hand. Although few people in the countryside go hungry, the standard of living of the rural community remains low.

Above: **Corn is one of the main staples in East African countries.**

Opposite: **Men preparing battery plates.**

Many tribes live in areas that are too dry to farm, and so depend heavily on their livestock, especially goats and camels.

Although there are no plans to change this basic style of living, people are now being encouraged to grow crops to sell. Farmers living in the highlands often grow a few coffee plants.

As much as half the coffee grown in Kenya now comes from small farms. Money from these "cash crops" can help buy tools, lamps, blankets or clothing.

The government helps farmers by buying fertilizer, insecticide, or new strains of seed. Officials also visit the villages to introduce new farming techniques, advise about pest control, or plan irrigation projects.

Traditionally, a farmer would divide his land up among his sons. However, with Kenya's growing population, there is often not enough land to support all the people, so many young men have been forced to leave their homes to seek work in the cities.

CASH CROPS

The growing of crops to sell overseas is vital for Kenya's economy. These cash crops account for about 30% of the nation's gross national product. Coffee is the most important crop, followed by tea. These are both grown in the fertile highland region, where there are many large plantations. Even this fertile area can be affected by drought, and the harvest can decrease by thousands of tons in a bad year. However, in years when the Brazilian coffee crop is damaged by frost, Kenya enjoys an economic boom.

Diversifying the economy has become more important as the world price for coffee fluctuates unpredictably. One result of the decline in coffee prices has been an increase in tea growing. High quality Kenyan tea is particularly popular in Europe. Other export crops are less important than the main two. Pyrethrum, sugarcane, wheat, sisal (which is used for making ropes), and cotton are also exported, as are some fruits.

Tea pickers on a tea plantation, one of Kenya's most recent attempts to diversify its economy.

COFFEE

The coffee plant is an evergreen shrub that grows best at higher altitudes. In the wild it can grow up to 20 feet (six meters) tall, but on plantations it is usually pruned much shorter to make harvesting easier. Coffee plants did not grow in the wild in Kenya, but were introduced by the Europeans. A good coffee plant will produce about one and a half pounds of roasted coffee each year. It takes between three and five years to bear fruit, and then produces coffee for 10 to 15 years.

The coffee plant produces a berry that changes from green to yellow and finally, when it is ripe, to bright red. The berries ripen at different speeds. At harvest time, teams of pickers move along the rows of plants, removing the red beans but leaving the others. This careful method of picking is one reason why Kenyan coffee is considered to be of such high quality.

After being harvested, the berries are taken to the sorting yard where the sacks are emptied and any leaves, twigs, or green berries removed. The berries are then placed in a pulping machine where the flesh is stripped from the fruit. Each berry has two beans (seeds) and these are covered in a second skin. The beans are left in fermenting tanks for 12 to 36 hours to loosen the remaining husks. They are then washed and spread out to dry. At the drying racks, workers smooth the wet husks into a single layer so that they can dry properly. Following this process, the crop is sent to Nairobi. Here, the berries are extracted from the last of the husks and then sent to be auctioned.

INDUSTRY

Kenya has relatively little industry, and manufacturing, as at 1990, employed only 13.3% of the population. Altogether, industry accounts for 18% of the economy, compared with 26% in Britain and 34% in Japan.

Kenya has to import many items because of its lack of industry, which is a heavy burden for a poor country. Nearly one-third of the money Kenya spends overseas goes to buy motor vehicles, electrical goods, and other forms of machinery.

However, since independence, the government has invested considerable money in building new factories. The industrial sector has grown at twice the rate of other areas of the economy.

Today, Kenya makes textiles, clothing, cement, chemicals, paper, beverages, dairy products, and electrical equipment, and has a large food processing industry.

Although it does not have oil of its own, Kenya does have the capability to refine oil. Imported oil comes into Mombasa to be refined and then sold to other African countries, and is one of Kenya's more lucrative industries.

Masai dancers entertain tourists, Kenya's fastest growing source of foreign income.

TOURISM

In 1986, tourism overtook coffee as Kenya's number one source of foreign income. That year, Kenya attracted 400,000 visitors. Tourism employs 40,000 people, and there is a special college to train workers for jobs in hotels and travel agencies. Many people not directly involved also benefit from the overseas visitors. These include woodcarvers, shop owners, and taxi drivers. Some people are concerned that many tourists do not show respect for Kenyan culture, while many young Kenyans have learned to hustle tourists for money. Traditionally, tourism centers around safari trips to the game parks.

Kenya has many excellent hotels. Some of the best run are the lodges in the game parks. Many lodges are situated around a water hole or river, where the animals come right up to the hotel. In some lodges, they will leave food out to attract birds, crocodiles, or even leopards. Most game parks also have campsites where people can feel closer to nature.

So many tourists are visiting Kenya that they are causing a problem in some game parks. In Amboseli National Park, minibuses were doing so much damage to the soil that all vehicles had to be restricted to the marked roads. Some drivers try to get their guests as close to the animals as possible, and in doing so often scare predators like cheetahs away from their kill, stopping the animals from feeding properly.

Few people wish to spend all their time in the game parks, so many trips combine a safari with a beach holiday. Lamu Island is a favorite spot for budget travelers, who often stay for several weeks to enjoy the friendly Arab culture. However, the tourist industry can be very vulnerable. There have been occasional attacks by animals on tourist buses in some game parks. News of this can cause hundreds of people to cancel their vacations. On the other hand, the release of a movie such as *Out of Africa* can result in thousands of people selecting Kenya for their next vacation.

On safari in the Tsavo National Park.

Buyers and sellers bargain at a market. The market is also a good place to go to exchange local news and gossip.

THE EAST AFRICAN COMMUNITY

Before independence, Kenya, Tanzania, and Uganda were all governed by Britain. Under colonial rule, these three countries shared the same tax system, had one customs service, one postal and communications service, and operated a joint railway company and airline. In addition, English and Swahili were common languages in all three countries, making trade and business simple. It was, therefore, natural that these close ties should continue after independence.

On December 1, 1967, the Treaty of East African Cooperation was signed, establishing an East African Community. Free trade was encouraged among the three partners, who agreed to combine many services and share the costs. Companies such as East African Airways were jointly owned and, for a while, the whole region benefited from the union. However, Tanzania and Uganda began to feel that Kenya, as the most industrialized of the three nations, was gaining more than they were.

As the economy of Tanzania and Uganda declined, the two nations found it more difficult to pay their share of the community expenses. Soon, many of the organizations ran into financial difficulty. East African Airways faced particularly serious problems. In 1976, Kenya shut down the airline and seized most of the aircraft. After this, the relationship between Kenya and Tanzania became strained, and for several years the border was closed. When President Moi came to power, the situation improved. In the early 1980s the border with Tanzania was reopened.

In the late 1980s and early 1990s President Moi's government had a stormy relationship with the international monetary authorities that led to a break with the International Monetary Fund and the World Bank in 1993. The relationship improved the following year and Kenya was able to reschedule a large part of its considerable foreign debt as international confidence in Kenya's economy improved.

Nairobi office workers enjoy the increased wealth the East African Community has given to the people.

KENYANS

THE SIZE AND SHAPE OF MODERN KENYA was determined by its European colonial rulers. As a result, Kenya today is made up of hundreds of different tribal groups, often with their own languages and culture. In other parts of Africa, this diversity has led to serious political problems and even wars. Aware of this danger, the Kenyan government has attempted to build a national identity under the motto *harambee*.

Some tribes, particularly the Kikuyu and Luo, have adopted many Western ways and fashions. Others groups, such as the Masai and Boran, have largely retained their traditional lifestyles.

Kenyan tribes are generally categorized into three main groups, according to the type of language they speak. These three groups are the Bantu, Cushitic, and Nilotic people.

Opposite: **A Turkana nomad from a tribe famous for its large and ornate jewelry.**

Left: **Kenyan descendents from different tribes on a sidewalk in Kenyatta Avenue, Nairobi.**

Some Kikuyu children.

THE BANTU PEOPLE

The Bantu speaking people are the largest group of Kenya's many tribes. They were originally from West Africa, probably an area around the Congo. They occupied the upper regions of Lake Victoria, central Kenya, and the southern coastal area. Today, they make up about 60% of Kenya's population. Within the Bantu group there are many different tribes, the largest of which are the Kikuyu, Luhya, and Kamba.

The Kikuyu tribe, who are traditionally a farming people, moved into the area around Mount Kenya about 400 years ago. They were never united into a large political group, but were governed by local councils of elders. They were among the first tribes to have contact with the Europeans, and many Kikuyu people lost their land to white farmers. However, the Kikuyu were some of the first Kenyans to accept Western education and modern ideas. As a result, despite not being in government, they are now the most influential group in Kenya. Many now live and work in the cities.

The Luhya ("LOO-ee-ah") are one of the largest of all the Kenyan tribes and number between 2 and 3 million people. However, they consist of 17 different groups, and there is some debate as to which groups should really be classified as members of the tribe.

The Maragoli ("mahr-ah-GO-lee"), for example, are usually considered part of the Luhya but they themselves dispute this, claiming to be totally separate. The Luhya come from the heavily populated western part of Kenya, so many have moved to Nairobi and elsewhere to seek work. They are noted for their pottery and basket weaving.

The Kamba ("KAM-bah") are another large Bantu tribe. They live in the dry lands between Nairobi and the coast and number about 2 million. Formerly hunters, most now make their living as herders or farmers. At the end of the last century, the Kamba economy was shattered by an outbreak of rinderpest (an infectious disease causing fever and dysentery) that killed many of their cattle. Poor farming practices and the cutting down of forests and bush to make charcoal have added to their poverty.

A Kikuyu child in a Mombasa doorway.

Tall Masai tribesmen, gathered in colorful attire.

THE NILOTIC TRIBES

About 600 years ago, the Nilotic tribes migrated to Kenya from the north. Their original home was in the Sudan, probably from an area close to the River Nile. Some of Kenya's most traditional tribes, such as the Masai and Samburu, belong to the Nilotic group.

The Luo are the largest and most influential of the Nilotic tribes. They were traditionally herders, but many settled around Lake Victoria and became fisherman. Others found their new home more suitable to farming. They number around 2 million people and, like the Kikuyu, have successfully adopted Western lifestyle and ideas. Many Luo have moved to the cities where they have become mechanics, machinists, and traders. As a result, the Luo are a powerful force in the trade unions.

They also played an important part in the independence struggle. Tom Mboya, vice president under Kenyatta, was a member of the Luo tribe. When Mboya was assassinated, it further fueled the rivalry between Kenya's two largest ethnic groups, the Bantu and Nilotic peoples.

The Nilotic Tribes

In sharp contrast to the Luo, the Masai are a very traditional people who have largely ignored the modern world. Although they are a relatively small tribe, perhaps numbering less than 250,000, they have become one of the best known ethnic groups in Africa. They tend to be a tall, slender, handsome people with a reputation for being fierce warriors.

Much of the work in Masai society is done by the women, for the men traditionally save their energy for defending the village and raiding other tribes. Today, even the Masai are accepting some changes in their lifestyle. Some Masai children attend school. Visits from veterinarians have helped combat disease among the cattle. There are also new problems. Now that cattle raids have been outlawed, Masai men have lost their main role within the tribe. This has created serious social tensions, including increased alcohol abuse.

A Masai warrior wearing an ostrich feather head-dress.

Two Boran women wearing aluminum jewelry.

THE CUSHITIC TRIBES

The Cushitic people are Kenya's third major tribal group. The tribes divide into two branches: the Oromo who came from Ethiopia, and the Somali who migrated from Somalia. These two groups of Cushitic people occupy a vast area of north and northeast Kenya. This is an extremely dry region that is often subject to drought and famine.

Most of the Cushitic people are herders of sheep, goats, and camels. The Somali tribe number around 400,000. They crossed the Juba River about 150 years ago, driving out the small hunter-gatherer tribes they met there.

The main Oromo tribes are the Boran, Gabbra, and Orma. The Orma, sometimes known as the Galla tribe, are a tall, slender people. They occupy the land on either side of the Tana River. Because this is more fertile than the surrounding arid land, they are able to keep herds of cattle and are famous for their long-horned Zebu-type cows. Within the Cushitic speaking people are also some of Kenya's smallest and most primitive tribes. These include the El Molo ("el MO-lo") and Boni.

THE OUTSIDERS

Apart from the African tribes, Kenya has small minority groups from other parts of the world. The first Arab traders came to Kenya nearly 1,000 years ago, and so have long ties with this region. Most Kenyan Arabs still live near the coast. With their bazaars and mosques, certain areas of Mombasa look as if they belong in the Middle East rather than Africa. Many Arabs are still involved in trading, while others make a living fishing.

Kenya also has a large number of people who originate from the Indian subcontinent. These people are generally referred to as Asians. At the turn of the century, thousands of Asians were brought to Kenya to work on the railway. Many stayed, often taking positions in the government or becoming traders. Today, the Asian community is still heavily involved in commerce and trading, although many now work in professions such as accountancy, medicine, engineering, or law.

A large number of Europeans fled Kenya when it became independent, but those who remained have generally fared well. Only Kenyans may own land, but all residents, whatever their color or background, were offered Kenyan citizenship. Some of the white Kenyans who remained are still prosperous farmers. However, the majority are expatriates, working on short-term contracts.

The white settlers in Kenya generally enjoy a very high standard of living. Here, a group enjoys a sumptuous dinner.

believe in communion with the dead to seek advice on important decisions.

Tharaka

This tribe of around 10,000 people live on the low, hot plains east of Mount Kenya. This is a harsh area, with endemic illnesses such as malaria and sleeping sickness. The Tharaka ("tar-AHK-ah") are famous for their witchcraft and colorful drums. They are also renowned beekeepers.

CUSHITIC TRIBES
Boni

The Boni live in the coastal hinterland and number around 5,000 people. They were originally hunter-gatherers and ivory traders. Today, they are involved in farming, but also collect honey and wild fruit, and hunt small animals.

El Molo

A tribe of a few hundred people who originally lived on two small islands in Lake Turkana. Fish form their basic diet, supplemented with crocodile meat. Some scientists think the El Molo might be descendants of the original inhabitants of Kenya.

NILOTIC TRIBES
Ilchamus

Although related to the Masai, the Ilchamus ("il-KAM-oos") mainly farm and fish. Numbering around 7,000 people, they live along the shores of Lake Baringo. They are noted for their exciting dances.

Nandi

The Nandi take their name from their beautiful Nandi Hills home. They moved there between

REMAINING SMALLER TRIBES

BANTU TRIBES
Senguju

The Senguju ("sen-GOO-joo"), like the Masai, were traditionally a warlike tribe owning vast herds of cattle. The Senguju have migrated south from their original home around Mount Kenya. Today, fewer than a thousand of them remain in Kenya, the rest having settled in Tanzania.

Taita and Taveta

These two tribes number around 16,000 people who farm the fertile Taita ("TAI-tah") Hills. Their traditional religion is very complex; they

300 and 400 years ago, and learned farming from the neighboring tribes. Previous to this, they were fierce warriors.

Pokot

This tribe of around 200,000 people live in the Great Rift Valley. Those living in the hills tend to be farmers, and those on the plains, cattle herders. The search for water and grazing often brings them into contact with the Turkana, and cattle raids still occur between the tribes.

Samburu

The Samburu number around 70,000 people, and live in the highlands around Mount Nyiru and on the arid plain below. In physical appearance and dress, the Samburu look very much like the Masai. However, they tend to be less warlike, and have become farmers of the fertile highlands.

Turkana

This large tribe of 300,000 people live in the parched north of Kenya along the shores of Lake Turkana. Until recently, this was a very remote area, and the Turkana remain one of the most primitive tribes in Kenya. Their economy is centered on cattle and camels, but they also fish in Lake Turkana.

LIFESTYLE

TRADITIONAL WAYS are slowly dying out in Kenya. First the missionaries and now the modern government have attempted to introduce new ideas and change some of the traditional customs. In some cases, this is probably for the best.

For example, in the past, twins and children born feet first were considered bad omens and might have been left to die. Fortunately, these kinds of practices have died out. However, other changes, particularly the breakdown of family ties, have created many new problems.

THE ROLE OF THE FAMILY

Kenyan society has traditionally revolved around the family. The term *family* is often used very broadly, and may be stretched to include cousins, uncles, or even more distant relations. Indeed, in cities, the help and support shown to the family is often extended to anybody from the same village, or even the same tribe. People who move to urban areas usually try to send money home to support people in the village.

Old people hold honored positions and are cared for and respected in Kenyan society. Traditionally, important decisions were always made at a gathering of the elder men of the village. However, in modern Kenya, such power has passed to government-appointed officials.

Above: **A Turkana family gathers at sunrise. The family unit is very important in Kenyan society.**

Opposite: **A woman making pots.**

Two Masai *moran* warriors.

PUBERTY

When children reach puberty, most tribes will traditionally circumcise both boys and girls. This is a sign that boys have reached manhood and that girls can now be married and bear children. Boys will usually go through the operation between the ages of 12 and 15. They will be expected to endure it without showing any sign of pain. Circumcision is particularly dangerous for girls, and the government is trying to stop this practice. However, many rural people are resisting this challenge to one of their oldest traditions, and refuse to change.

Before and after the circumcision, there is a period of seclusion. The young people are considered to leave the village as children, but return "reborn" as adults. Young women in the Pokot tribe gather for several weeks of seclusion, and receive advice and instruction from older women. On the day of the operation, they place chalk on their faces and wear loose robes to hide their identities. Following this, they marry.

In some societies, the circumcision ceremony initiates the boys into the warrior stage of their lives. Masai boys are taken away from the village for several days, during which they are dressed in women's robes. When they return, they have their heads shaved and are recognized as men. They are known as *moran*, and are forced out of the security of their homes to live in rough camps with other young men their own age.

Wealthier people have their children circumcised in hospitals, but often the operation is conducted in the traditional way by people with no medical training. Under these circumstances, infections are common.

BIRTH

Birth is considered a great occasion, and the mother-to-be is attended by several midwives. Some tribes carry the afterbirth out to the fields and bury it. This is thought to appease the gods and ensure that the land remains fertile.

The birth is often followed by a period of seclusion. When the mother emerges from her home to show the new baby to her friends, a goat might be sacrificed and a feast held. The arrival of a new baby is seen as an event for the whole village to celebrate.

For the parents, a baby girl brings the promise of future wealth, as daughters can bring a marriage dowry. Sons are believed carry the spirits of the ancestors and form a link with the past.

The prestige of the new parents also increases. The father of the child might gain a higher level of elderhood. In villages where medical assistance is primitive, many babies still die at birth.

A teacher supervising school children. Literacy in Kenya is on the increase.

EDUCATION

Many Kenyans now place considerable importance on education. Elementary education is provided free by the government, but attendance is not compulsory. Many schools insist that children buy uniforms and books, so families have to save in order to send their children to school.

Since 1985, Kenya has adopted an eight-year elementary school, four-year high school, and four-year college system. The main subjects studied are arithmetic, geography, Swahili, and hygiene. English is taught at the high school level. There are exams for entering high school and college, and competition is tough. In the cities, there are many private schools that sometimes offer better facilities to those who can afford them.

HEALTH

Health care has improved considerably since independence. There are good hospitals in the cities, although the best are private and expensive. There are clinics in most villages, and progress has been made in providing clean water and preventive medical education.

The life expectancy in Kenya is around 52 years for men and 55 for women. This is well below American or European standards, but better than many other African countries. Malaria is a great danger in many regions, and worm infestations and bilharzia are common. Even diseases such as leprosy and sleeping sickness are still present.

As Kenyans live longer and become more affluent, "Western" problems of obesity and heart disease are also becoming more common.

A Turkana nomad bride—
the extent of her necklace
indicates her husband's
wealth.

MARRIAGE

Most tribal cultures demand a "bride price" that is paid by the husband's family to the family of the bride. Traditionally, this would be paid in cattle or animal stock. However, today, this dowry may be in cash or electrical goods. The bride price system means that many marriages are arranged by the families, and the young people's feelings toward each other are not always taken into account. Once the union has been agreed, a feast will be arranged at the husband's house, after which the couple are acknowledged as married.

Today, many Kenyans have a Christian wedding in a church. Such an event would be very similar to that celebrated in the West.

It is still common for Kenyan men to take more than one wife. It is a man's duty to provide a separate home for each wife, often many miles apart. In such marriages, there is a strong hierarchy among the wives, with the senior wife usually enjoying more authority and influence. The first wife may even have a say in selecting other wives. In many ways, polygamy is intended as an insurance policy. Each wife looks after a proportion of her husband's animals, so that if there is an outbreak of disease, the family might not lose all its herds.

Education has made many young women question the traditional practices of polygamy and arranged marriages. In addition, new economic pressures, particularly the lack of land, means fewer men are wealthy enough to support more than one wife.

THE ROLE OF WOMEN IN KENYA

Kenya, like most African nations, is a male-dominated society. It has been suggested that African women do 80% of the work, but receive almost none of the money. In the village, a woman's work may include helping with the farming, selling the surplus crops in the market, and all the fetching and carrying. Many homes are without a convenient water supply, so thousands of women have to carry heavy containers of water home from the nearest well. In most families, the man controls the money. For many women, the only hope of progress is to find a husband with either land or a good job. But divorce is still something to be feared, since it could leave them penniless.

Conditions are slowly improving for women, and they now have a far better chance of acquiring an education. As a result, they are beginning to participate more in commerce and other professions. A few women, such as Phoebe Asiyo, have even been elected to Parliament.

Kamba people plowing with oxen. Farming methods are still very traditional in Kenya.

IN THE VILLAGE

Life in a typical village revolves around the crops. Generally, people go to bed early and wake up at sunrise. After working in the fields, the men spend the evening talking and exchanging stories. Occasionally, the whole family makes a trip into town to buy items such as blankets, lamps, or tools.

People in the countryside offer each other considerable assistance. When a man has a difficult job, he can expect all his relatives and neighbors to help. In return, he is obliged to assist other people when asked.

Traditionally, land was divided among the sons. With the ever increasing population, this is becoming impractical. Many young people now go to the city to seek work. In addition, young men who have received an education are often reluctant to take over the family plot, preferring instead to seek employment in the city.

IN THE CITY

For rich Kenyans, city life offers a similar standard of living to that in the West. The richest Kenyans are often mockingly called *wabenz* ("wa-BENZ") due to their preference for Mercedes Benz cars. It is considered important in urban society to demonstrate one's status and success.

By contrast, vast numbers of urban Kenyans are either unemployed or can find only occasional work. For these unfortunate people, life in the city can be dismal. In Nairobi, enormous shanty towns have appeared where people live in houses made of discarded junk, without electricity or water. Many try hard to find a job. Some are reduced to begging while others turn to crime.

However, even if they do find a poorly paid job, they often earn more money than they would have in the village.

Workers walk home along City Hall Way, Nairobi.

RELIGION

KENYA HAS NO STATE RELIGION, and people are free to worship in any way they wish. Many Kenyans have converted to Christianity, and a smaller number to Islam. However, the old tribal beliefs have survived in many communities, and in times of difficulty, even Christians sometimes turn to the tribal beliefs for help.

TRIBAL RELIGIONS

Some 18% of Kenyans still follow an animistic religion. Although different from tribe to tribe, the basic belief is that every natural object, natural phenomenon, and even the universe itself possesses a soul or spirit. Such spirits are capable of influencing the human world and so must be worshiped or appeased. Spirits might also occasionally "possess" somebody. When a person is believed to be possessed by a spirit that is not friendly, an exorcism will be performed.

Opposite: **A medicine man casts spells to ward off evil spirits.**

Left: **A Christian church at Horr in northern Kenya.**

ONE GOD

Another factor common to nearly every tribal religion is the belief in a single great founder and creator of all things. The creator's name varies from tribe to tribe, but it is often known as Mulungu ("moo-LOON-goo").

The Kikuyu call the creator Ngai ("n-GAI"). They believe he chose a man named Gikuyu to be the father of the Kikuyu people, and gave him Mumbi as a wife. Gikuyu was taken to a high mountain and shown all the land around. He was told to go and populate this land. Gikuyu and Mumbi produced nine daughters, but no sons. So the couple returned to Ngai, who created nine husbands for their daughters. These couples founded the nine clans of the Kikuyu people.

The magnificent Mount Kilimanjaro, seen by East African people as the seat of the gods.

The Masai also call the creator of the world Ngai, and believe he left Earth to go and live in the sky above Mount Kilimanjaro. They believe it was Ngai who gave the Masai their cattle to sustain them. The Masai have used this belief to justify raiding other people's cattle, saying that they are only reclaiming what Ngai intended for them.

TRADITIONAL WORSHIP

Many tribes attempt to contact the spirits through prayers. The Masai may pray at any time of the day, but sunrise is particularly favored. Masai women have special prayers for particular occasions. Some are for ceremony, others for times of drought. Some are also sung during storms to seek protection from lightning.

Religious celebrations and festivals, like most others in Kenya, involve dancing as a means of expression. These dancers are from the Kikuyu tribe.

African religions have produced virtually no temples or churches. However, the Kikuyu are one of the few African people to have sacred places. These are generally quiet, secluded spots where people may go in times of stress. Holy places are sometimes marked by small piles of stones.

The Kipsigis have a shrine in each homestead. They employ people they believe have special powers to communicate with their god during drought or illness, which the Kipsigis believe is not a punishment, but a warning from their god to undo their wrongs and repent.

Opposite: **A herbal doctor, one of the alternative sources Kenyans consult for medical cures.**

Below: **By contrast, the more traditional witch doctor.**

SPIRITS AND MAGIC

The creator is usually seen as a good god, and evil must therefore be the work of supernatural spirits that can bring disease, drought, or death.

This belief in the power of spirits has led Kenyan society to develop a variety of dances, animal sacrifices, and magic charms to ward off evil. At the same time, good magicians are respected, for they can protect a village and summon the rains.

There are several different categories of magicians. These include diviners, medicine men, and witch doctors. The role of each can vary from tribe to tribe, and even from village to village. Some magicians will claim a combination of these special gifts.

Diviners are believed to have the ability to peer into the spirit world. If troubled, a person can ask a diviner for help. The magical powers of the diviner enable him to locate the spirits that are causing the problem, and then suggest a magical cure. Diviners can also use the spirits to see into the future.

In his book, *Facing Mount Kenya,* Jomo Kenyatta relates the story of a wise Kikuyu man who, in a vision, saw the coming of the pale-faced Europeans with their guns and railways.

The Masai have their own fortune-tellers, whom they call *laibon* ("LAIbon"). One method of fortune-telling is to read the message in pebbles cast from a gourd. The services of the *laibon* may be used to settle family disputes or, in the past, to predict the success of a cattle raid.

There are also medicine men or women who understand traditional medicines, and are experts in diagnosing problems and offering a cure. Some of the potions they offer make use of healing herbs, but much of their craft involves the use of magic. They offer cures for problems beyond the normal realms of medical treatment.

Many people still believe that witchcraft can be used to cause illness, bad luck, or death. Witches or sorcerers are people born with the magical power of diviners, but who misuse that power against their neighbors. Witch doctors are employed to detect witches.

There are various ways of seeking out a witch. Under the direction of their witch doctor, the Pokot tribe gather and share a brew with a "powerful medicine" in it. The brew will be harmful to the witch, but to no one else. Anybody not attending the ceremony, or refusing to drink, can be identified as the witch.

Some witch doctors have been known to offer cures and protection to a person who has had a curse placed on him·or her. The Kamba perform similar witch-cleansing ceremonies. They are particularly feared by other tribes for the powerful witchcraft they are reputed to possess.

CHRISTIANITY

The majority of Kenyans are Christians. Christianity was brought to Africa by European missionaries. The African people had little problem assimilating their own belief in a supreme being with the Christian concept of God. However, Christianity faced many other conflicts with traditional practices, particularly polygamy. In most Kenyan societies, men were encouraged to take more than one wife. This was seen as a sign of wealth and brought considerable prestige within the community.

Despite such differences, Christianity has had considerable success in gaining converts among agricultural people such as the Kikuyu. By contrast, the cattle herding tribes such as the Masai have largely resisted the faith.

Some Christians worshiping under a tree—an example of how the animistic tribal religious practices have mixed with Christian beliefs.

The Kenyan church has always been involved in politics. At first, the church helped the colonial authorities control the African population. But during the 1950s, an increasing number of African pastors supported the call for independence in their sermons. Today, the church is one of the strongest voices in demanding more democracy for Kenya.

The traditional church is often seen as a legacy of European rule, and many groups have broken away to found their own churches. Such "African" churches are often far more sympathetic to indigenous beliefs or customs. Many of these churches will accept polygamous marriages and hold circumcision services.

The largest independent church is the Church of Christ in Africa, with its cathedral in Nairobi. It aims much of its teaching at the urban poor, and offers traditional education and healing to the poor and needy.

THE MISSIONARIES

During the 19th century, there was a powerful movement in Europe to convert the world to Christianity. Africa became a favorite destination for enthusiastic young missionaries. It was believed that commerce, civilization, and Christianity should be used to educate the Africans and bring them into the mainstream of world events.

The first missionaries arrived in Kenya around 1844 and slowly spread inland to the Rift Valley. They offered training in farming, crafts, and health care. Because it was necessary to read the Bible to understand Christianity, the church also established the first schools.

Many Kenyans were genuinely interested in the faith. At the same time, newly educated Kenyans saw Christianity as a useful way of improving their fortunes. As a result of these influences, the Christian church became powerful.

Despite the missionaries' good work, critics now look back on them and recognize that they were often very arrogant and insensitive to the local traditions and culture. These missionaries might also have done far more to protect the African people's civil rights.

OTHER RELIGIONS

About 6% of Kenya's population are Muslim. These people live mainly on the coast where there has long been a powerful Arabic influence.

However, one finds large mosques in Nairobi and in most other major inland towns. Many of the Somali-speaking people are also Muslims, as are a small section of the Asian community.

Most of the Asian community are Hindus and have their own temples. The Hindu religion has had little impact on the African population, and there has been no attempt to convert people.

There are other small groups, such as the Sikhs and Jains, as well as Indians from Goa who follow the Roman Catholic faith.

A Jain temple in Mombasa.

LANGUAGE

ALTHOUGH SCHOLARS can identify the various Bantu people from the similarities in their languages, the different Bantu tribes are not necessarily able to understand each other. Each ethnic group has developed its own version of the language, and these can be as different as English is from German.

First the colonial powers and then the modern government encouraged the use of Kiswahili ("ki-swah-HEE-lee") as a common language. However, English is also widely used and is the language of technology, higher education, medicine, business, and international trade.

THE SWAHILI PEOPLE

Swahili can refer to both the language and to some of the people who live along the Kenyan and Tanzanian coast. The Bajuni ("ba-JOON-i"), Swahili ("swah-HEE-lee"), and Shirazi ("shir-AHZ-ee") are the tribes who originally spoke Kiswahili.

The origins of these people are unknown, but they are probably descendants of immigrants from India and Persia who intermixed with tribes already living along the edge of the Indian Ocean. From the eighth century onward, this group in turn mixed with the Arab traders. By the twelfth century, the Swahili people had emerged as a distinct group.

The Swahili built several towns along the coast and on islands such as Lamu. Swahili towns often had palaces, forts, and mosques made from stone. They also produced written chronicles and minted coins.

Above: **A selection of Kenya's English language newspapers.**

Opposite: **A child learning the Koran.**

This Nairobi street sign illustrates the variety of languages to be found in modern Kenya.

KISWAHILI OR ENGLISH?

Kiswahili is the native language of a few small tribes who live along the coast. Because it was the language that the Arabs first came into contact with, it became the language used in trade. The Arab merchants spread the use of Kiswahili into the interior, where many people learned to speak at least a few words and phrases. It was therefore convenient for later governments to encourage the use of Kiswahili as the common language.

Today, most Kenyans can understand Kiswahili, but those using it as a second language often speak it very poorly. There are seven main dialects, but *kiunguja* ("kee-oon-GOO-jah"), which is spoken in Mombasa, is accepted as the standard version. In 1974, Kiswahili was officially adopted as the national language of Kenya. However, in practice, it really shares that role with English. For example, there are relatively few books being printed in Kiswahili, and anybody involved in higher education must learn English.

A CHANGING LANGUAGE

Over the years, Kiswahili has borrowed many "loan words" from other languages, particularly Arabic. The word *Swahili* is taken from the Arabic word *sawahil*, which means "coastal people." Arabic words were borrowed or adapted for items that the Africans had not seen before. These include words such as *kahawa,* meaning "coffee."

With the arrival of the Europeans, many additional new words were needed, and these were often an adaptation of the European word. For example, the Kiswahili word for bicycle is *baisikeli,* motor car is *moto kaa,* ticket is *tiketi,* and blanket is *blanketi.*

Portuguese and German words can also be found in the language. This loaning of words has not been a one-way process. Kiswahili has given to the world such words as impala and safari, both now established in the English language.

Children learning English at Hospital Hill School in Nairobi.

WRITING IT DOWN

Kiswahili was one of the first written African languages. Many centuries ago, the early Arab settlers were using their own script to write chronicles in Kiswahili. Today, Kiswahili is usually written using the Latin alphabet.

The missionaries developed grammar and spelling rules for recording Kiswahili, based on those of the European languages. This work forms the basis of today's accepted style, which is known as East African Standard.

This style is used not only in Kenya, but also in Uganda and Tanzania. Over 50 million people now speak and write Kiswahili in this form, so it can be considered one of the major African languages.

OTHER TRIBAL LANGUAGES

It is estimated that there are about 80 major languages in Kenya. The spoken dialect often changes slowly from one village to the next until, over a distance of many miles, a new language seems to emerge.

A Muslim boy learns the Koran.

A bookshop in Nairobi.

Most Kenyan languages have grown out of Bantu, Nilotic, or Cushitic languages. Kiswahili is considered a Bantu language, although it has many later influences. Kenyan writers are concerned that the extensive use of English in literature will both limit their audience and lead to a decline in tribal languages. Kenya's most famous writer, Ngugi wa Thiong'o, pioneered the use of Africa's own tribal languages, and many writers since have followed his example. *Voice of Kenya* now broadcasts many regional programs in the local languages of the respective areas.

Many Kenyans speak more than one language. Most know their own tribal language and Kiswahili. Those with a high school education, or involved in business, will almost certainly speak English. Many people also know the tribal language of their trading neighbors.

KISWAHILI WORDS AND EXPRESSIONS

Probably the first word any visitor hears in Kiswahili is *jambo* ("JAM-boh"), meaning "hello." When speaking to a man, it is polite to address him as *bwana* ("BWAH-nah"), a contraction of *baba wa wana*, meaning "the father of many sons." A young man talking to an old man should address him as *mzee*. On entering a house, you will likely be greeted with *karibuni* ("kar-i-BOON-ee"), which means "welcome." *Asante* ("ah-SAN-tay") means "thank you," and is often used with *sana*—"thank you very much." The word *harambee* ("pull together") has a deeper meaning in Kenyan culture, as does *uhuru* ("oo-HOO-roo"), which means "independence."

Sentences and expressions are often built up around a root word. For example, *penda* is the word for "like." *Kupenda* means "to like." If you want to say "I like," it would be *ninapenda*. *Ninamupenda* means "I like you" and translates word for word as "I-you-like."

Telling the time is very different in Kiswahili. The Swahili people measure the start of the day from when the sun rises at 6 a.m. What we know as 7 a.m. is therefore 1 p.m. Kiswahili time, or the end of the first hour of the morning. Night begins when the sun sets.

A LAND OF MANY LANGUAGES

Although most of the African countries had gained independence from the European colonial powers of the nineteenth century by the 1960s, the languages that were brought with the Europeans remain throughout Africa. These European languages, mainly English and French, serve today as both languages of administration and common national languages.

Africa has a long history of importing languages and as a result has a large number of language and dialect groups. There are, for example, almost 900 Niger-Congo languages spoken across Africa from Mauritania to Kenya.

KENYAN NAMES

During colonial times, Africans who were baptized often took European names. President Kenyatta himself used the name Johnstone Kamu when he attended missionary school. Later, on entering politics, he reverted to the African name of Jomo Kenyatta.

European names such as David, Stephen, William, Susan, and Mary are still common in Kenya. In addition, some English names that have since gone out of fashion in the rest of the world remain popular. Julius, Wilfred, and Wilberforce are examples of this. Biblical names, such as Moses or Jonah, are also widely used.

However, an increasing number of Kenyans are choosing African names. Traditional names include Simba, Maganga, and Yobes.

Islamic names are very popular with the Muslim population in the country. So it is not unusual to find Kenyans called Ibrahim, Salim, or Mohammed.

THE NUMBERS

1 – *moja*		8	– *nane*
2 – *mbili*		9	– *tisa*
3 – *tatu*		10	– *kumi*
4 – *nne*		11	– *kumi na moja* (10 + 1)
5 – *tano*		13	– *kumi na tatu* (10 + 3)
6 – *sita*		100	– *mia moja*
7 – *saba*		110	– *mia moja na kumi* (100 + 10)

ARTS

MUSIC AND DANCE are the most important forms of artistic expression in traditional Kenyan society. Both have a religious significance, and are often used as a means to contact the spirit world.

Storytelling was also very important, although prior to the arrival of the Arabs and Europeans, there was no way to record the Kenyan tales.

Today, more and more people are becoming aware of the importance of Kenya's cultural heritage. But at the same time, the country is becoming increasingly influenced by Western music, literature, and art.

TRADITIONAL DANCE AND MUSIC

Each ethnic group has its own music, which has been used in rituals that have survived for centuries. Much of Kenyan music is "polyrhythmic," which means that different instruments play in different rhythms at the same time.

The key element in traditional Kenyan music are the large drums called *ngoma* ("n-GO-mah"). These drums are often made from hollowed-out sections of tree trunks with a skin stretched over the top. Zebra skin is traditionally considered the best to use for drums.

Large and ornate horns may also be used to accompany a dance or story. Flutes made from bamboo or some other hollow plant are another traditional wind instrument. They are usually used to accompany stories rather than dance.

Above: **Kenyans playing the *ngoma* at a festival.**

Opposite: **A colorfully dressed Samburu warrior.**

Kenyan tribes have also developed some string instruments. At the most simple level, there is the single-string bow. This probably developed from the hunting bow. African lyres are considerably more advanced instruments. They are often used to accompany singing in festivals and magical rites. One of the largest lyres is the *obukano* ("o-boo-KAHN-o"), a large bow-shaped instrument that has been described as "the double bass of Africa."

The *mbira* ("m-BIR-ah"), an instrument found only in Africa, is also popular in Kenya. The *mbira* is a box with narrow bands of metal fixed at one end, each strip of metal tuned to a different pitch. To produce a tune these bands are "twanged," usually with the thumb. The *mbira* is found all over Africa and is known by several names, including *sansa* or *kalimba*. Sometimes they are even referred to as "thumb pianos" or "finger xylophones."

A Kisii tribesman playing a local form of guitar.

Traditionally, African music's most important role was to accompany dances. Such music relied heavily on rhythm that could be produced by hitting sticks, stamping feet, clapping, or beating on a drum.

Most dances originally had some spiritual meaning. Some might be for fertility, others to ask the spirits to grant a good harvest or bring rain. Today, some dance troupes retain the traditional style and costume. Others have adapted modern ideas and might wear specially designed T-shirts and use whistles to accompany the music. However, these changes are a sign that dance is alive and adapting to the modern world.

THE STORYTELLERS

Storytellers can still make a living by traveling from village to village entertaining people with their folk tales. A story might last for hours—which seems strange to us but is, after all, no longer than an average-length movie. To hold an audience's attention for so long, the storyteller needs humor and stage presence. The ability to speak well is highly respected in Kenyan culture.

Many of Kenya's folk tales have animals as the main characters. The hare is a favorite hero of Kikuyu stories and will outwit the stronger lions and hyenas. The slow-moving tortoise often appears as another hero. Such tales usually have a strong moral line, with the cheating villains coming to some dreadful end.

Poetry might also be used to entertain people, and can be recited or sung. The coastal Swahili people are particularly noted for their poetry. This is probably a result of Arab influence.

Masai warriors perform their famous traditional jumping dance.

MODERN WRITERS

The first Kenyan writers tended to produce autobiographies that described village life. Jomo Kenyatta's *Facing Mount Kenya* was one of the first such books. From the 1950s onward, such autobiographical accounts tended to concentrate on the independence struggle and the Mau Mau uprising. Most of the earlier writers were from the Kikuyu tribe, although Grace Ogot wrote some excellent accounts of life in a Luo community.

The best known Kenyan writer, and the first to write novels, is Ngugi wa Thiong'o. As a boy, Ngugi wa Thiong'o was inspired by the storytellers who visited his village. They were a major influence on his writing career. His first novel, *Weep Not, Child,* was published in 1964. It told of the conflict within a Kikuyu family divided by the Mau Mau rebellion. His best known book, *Petals of Blood*, was published in 1977. It contrasts the life of the poor villagers with that of the newly-rich and often corrupt Kenyans. When he wrote in English, Ngugi's ideas were tolerated by the government. However, in 1978, he took up similar themes in a play, *I Will Marry When I Want*, written and performed in the Kikuyu language. As a result, the author spent a year in jail, but was released when President Moi came to power.

Meji Mwangi emerged in the 1970s as another important Kenyan novelist. His first books, such as *Taste of Death,* described the heroic actions of the freedom fighters.

From the 1970s onward, Kenyan writers started to focus on the fate of poor people in the city. Around this time, an important author to emerge was Charles Mangua. His books took a more humorous and lighter look at life, although they still carried a serious message. His books, including *Son of Woman* and *A Tail in the Mouth*, have broken all sales records in Kenya.

Traditional tribal wood carvings, an example of Kenya's thriving art and craft industry.

Students practicing in a school play—drama is popular in modern Kenya.

KENYAN THEATER

Considering many traditional storytellers were such talented performers, it is perhaps surprising that no natural theater developed among Kenya's people. Instead, the concept of acting out a story was introduced to Kenya by the Europeans. At first, theater in Kenya was a "whites only" activity. However, the early schools soon introduced African children to plays and acting.

The Nairobi African Dramatic Society was formed in 1940, and there was a growth in African drama groups after independence. At first, the groups performed Western plays, but now they have the opportunity to perform locally written plays such as *The Trial Of Dedan Kimathi* and *The Black Hermit,* both by Ngugi wa Thiong'o.

There was also an attempt to form traveling theaters to take plays out into the countryside. This was very much a return to the tradition of the wandering storyteller. The Kamiriithu ("kah-mir-i-EET-hoo") Theater became a center for political dramas and protests about social conditions.

ART—TRADITIONAL AND MODERN

There is very little traditional art in East Africa and virtually none of what
the West calls "fine art." A few tribes take particular care with the carving
and decoration of everyday items, such as stools or wooden pillows.
Considerable work and skill may also go into the production of jewelry or
religious items, such as drums and dance masks. The Masai are particularly
noted for their bead jewelry.

Today, the tourist trade has created a large market for carvings. Animals
and human figures are favorite subjects, usually made from wood but
occasionally in other mediums. Although hand-carved, hundreds of very
similar pieces are produced to sell, and such work is not taken very
seriously by the carvers. The Kamba tribe, who in the past produced some
of the best drums and stools, create much of today's tourist art.

Some of the best Kamba carvers are beginning to experiment with
original ideas. Perhaps the most famous is Elkana Ong'esa, who creates
soapstone abstracts. One of his carvings stands outside the UNESCO
headquarters in Paris.

Kenya has a world renowned museum which contains collections of wildlife as well as archeological displays and cultural artifacts. The museum works in partnership with the university and they jointly conduct research into all aspects of Kenyan cultural history.

SOAPSTONE

Soapstone is a soft, smooth stone that can be easily carved. It comes in several colors, the most popular for carving being a dull shade of pink. Most of the stones are found in regions inhabited by the Kisii ("ki-SEE-ee") tribe, who have, naturally, become the best carvers. However, the Kamba are now purchasing soapstone, and are starting to produce some exciting works.

A typical carver has to cut his own stone from a quarry, and then carry it home. He carves it with a knife, polishes the carving with sandpaper, and cleans it with a brush. Almost all the statues are sold to tourists. Animals, fish, and birds are the favorite subjects.

A large statue can take up to three days to produce, while small animals may be finished in less than an hour. The carver either sells the pieces to a middleman in the village or, more likely, takes them himself to Mombasa or Nairobi and sells them to tourist shops. Several thousand Kisii make their living from carving soapstone, and are dependent on Kenya's tourism industry for a living.

MODERN MUSIC

Kenyans have long been exposed to Western music. Church choirs, school concerts, and military bands were early influences. The guitar has become the most popular instrument in modern Kenyan music.

The arrival of Western instruments gave African musicians a chance to experiment in a way that was often lacking in their own traditional music. Although the instruments and stage techniques have been borrowed from Europe, the music produced is often very original.

A group of Mombasa musicians playing at a wedding.

These days, most modern music, sometimes referred to as "town music," is a combination of traditional rhythms and Western rock. However, there are many other influences such as jazz, reggae, or Nigerian high life (a mixture of Western big-band sound and African rhythms). "Call and response" is a very popular style in which a chorus of voices responds to a caller. Songs are written in Swahili or English, or often a combination of the two. Many of the best bands in Kenya have Tanzanian or Zairian musicians performing in them.

There is an active live music scene, and a good band can draw large crowds to clubs or dance halls. Songwriters are generally careful to stay away from political themes, as the only way to attract a nationwide audience is to be given air time on the government-controlled radio stations.

With increasing exposure to Western ideas, the Kenyan music scene may be in danger of losing some of its own distinctive style and sound.

LEISURE

IN THE PAST, traditional leisure activities in Kenya centered on family and friends. On ceremonial occasions, dancing was the most important form of entertainment.

Today, this pattern is changing. Many Kenyans in the cities now enjoy taking part in sports or watching television. Nairobi and Mombasa offer excellent theaters, restaurants, and clubs.

LEISURE TIME IN THE VILLAGE

Kenyans love to socialize, tell stories, share experiences, or simply gossip. These often seem to be national pastimes.

There are a few simple games that are part of Kenya's traditional culture. One such game is a version of "jacks" that is played with stones. This is popular with children, as is checkers. Men are more likely to play *kigogo* ("ki-GO-go"). Children often amuse themselves without toys, and much of their play consists of simple activities such as running, climbing, and wrestling. Children who live by the sea or lakes are likely to spend hours playing in boats, fishing, or swimming.

However, boys today are equally likely to spend their leisure time playing soccer. Often a bundle of rags will be used for a ball, and in the countryside, any tree or even a termite's nest will serve as a goal post.

In the cities, especially Nairobi and the coastal region, a young person's leisure outside of the home revolves around the live music scene in the clubs and bars.

Opposite: **A group playing the popular *kigogo* game.**

KIGOGO

Kigogo, also known as *mancala,* is the most common board game in Africa. Rules vary from region to region, and the game is quite complicated. Basically, it involves picking up counters—usually seeds, stones, or shells—and distributing them around a board in a way that will "capture" the opponent's pieces. The board may be an elaborate wood carving with hollows to hold the pieces, or simply some squares scratched in the sand. Good *kigogo* players gain considerable respect and prestige within their community.

Women gather in a country market to practice one of Kenya's most popular pastimes: exchanging news.

The land is very important to the Kenyan people. In agricultural areas, young boys are encouraged to plant and tend small gardens. Among the pastoral tribes, very young boys spend long hours tending the herds. Often there is little to do, so they may pass their time throwing stones and spears. These are important skills to learn, for in such societies, young men are still respected for their skill as warriors. For both boys and men, the time spent herding cattle is a good opportunity to practice musical instruments and sing traditional songs.

Some leisure activities are specific to certain tribes. The Embu people, for example, are skilled stilt walkers, and this forms an important part of their dance productions. To acquire this skill, Embu children must spend many hours playing on stilts. The people living on the shores of Lake Victoria organize canoe races, whose basic elements have been borrowed from modern sports.

Kenyans in the most arid areas have a bitter struggle to survive during much of the year. Only after a good rainy season is there any opportunity to relax and enjoy a little leisure time. This is the time for weddings and ceremonies, and these will be accompanied by dancing and feasts.

Larger towns offer more organized recreation. Scouting is a popular activity in Kenya. The founder of the Boy Scouts, Baden Powell, is buried in Kenya, and the scout troop of Nyeri ("nai-AIR-ee") has the honor of keeping his grave weeded and tidy.

Each year, more and more radios and television sets can be found in the villages. An increasing number of people are using their leisure time to listen to music, stories, and news from around the world.

A young Kikuyu girl looks after her little brother. It is said that Kenyan girls never need dolls, because they always have younger brothers and sisters to tend.

THE BEST RUNNERS IN THE WORLD

Kenyan long-distance runners are among the finest in the world. The country has produced a long list of Olympic champions. The Kipsigis and Nandi both have a reputation for producing great runners. Nobody is quite sure why these small ethnic groups have been able to produce so many world-class athletes. Living at high altitudes is probably a factor. Many Kenyan athletes say they became strong runners by having to jog several miles to school each day, so lifestyle may be another major influence.

Kenya's international success started with Wilson Kiprugut. In 1964, he became the first black African to win an Olympic track medal when he finished third in the 800 meters. Four years later, the Olympic team did even better, winning four gold medals in Mexico.

In middle- and long-distance running, Kenya has been a major sports power for the last three decades.

Kenya did not go to the 1976 Olympics. The African countries were angry that New Zealand was still maintaining sporting links with South Africa, and they decided to boycott the Olympics as a protest. It was a great disappointment for the athletes, but many of them continued training and hoped to make up for the missed opportunity in 1980. However, after the former Soviet Union invaded Afghanistan, Kenya again boycotted the Games. This meant that a whole generation of Kenyan athletes never had the opportunity to prove themselves in the Olympics.

In 1984 Kenya resumed participation in the Olympic Games and its athletes have done better in each subsequent competition. One medal was won in 1984 for the steeplechase; five medals were won in 1988 in track events, steeplechase, and boxing; and in 1992 Kenya won a record eight medals. At that Olympiad two Kenyan runners took the gold and silver medals in the 800 meter run and Kenyans won all three medals in the men's 3000 meter steeplechase. Other medals were won for the 5000 meter and 10,000 meter runs.

The growing popularity of the marathon has enabled many Kenyans to compete for large prize money. Douglas Wakiihuri is the best known Kenyan marathon runner, but his story is quite unusual. Although born in Kenya, he did not take up running seriously until he went to Japan as a student. Many other Kenyans have used their athletic ability to gain scholarships to American colleges.

Every year there is a world championship for cross country runners, and Kenya has dominated this event. John Ngugi won the individual race four years in a row and is regarded as one of the great distance runners in modern sport. Kenya continues to improve in the sporting arena and in some events is setting the world standard for performance.

KIP KEINO – THE FIRST OF THE GREAT RUNNERS

Kip Keino is still the most famous African athlete of all time. He won four Olympic medals—two of them gold—and broke two world records. He will always be remembered for his remarkable versatility and his friendly and modest personality.

Keino was born in a small village close to the Ugandan border. He did not take up running until he was 22, but in his very first year of serious competition, he was selected for the Kenyan team that went to the 1964 Commonwealth Games.

By the following year, Keino had matured into a truly great runner. During a tour of Australia, he broke the world records for the 3,000 and 5,000 meters. The next year, 1966, brought his first major successes and he won two gold medals at the Commonwealth Games. Keino was now a national hero and was given a job in the police force. Like many Kenyans, Keino was a natural athlete, and his European and American rivals were always amazed at how little training he seemed to need.

Keino entered three events at the 1968 Olympics and, despite stomach problems, came away with two medals. In the last event, the 1,500 meters, he scored a spectacular victory over the world record holder and favorite, Jim Ryan. It was a doubly happy day for Keino, for back in Kenya, his wife gave birth to a baby daughter.

Four years later, Keino won a second Olympic gold medal, this time in the steeplechase, an event he seldom entered. Unlike today's athletes, Keino never gained much financial reward from his running. After the 1972 Olympics, he returned to Kenya and slipped from the spotlight.

Career details:
1962: 3 miles, 11th, Commonwealth Games
1965: 5,000 meters, World Record
1965: 3,000 meters, World Record
1966: 3 miles, Gold medal, Commonwealth Games
1966: 1 mile, Gold medal, Commonwealth Games
1968: 5,000 meters, Silver medal, Olympics
1968: 1,500 meters, Gold medal, Olympics
1970: 1,500 meters, Gold medal, Commonwealth Games
1972: 1,500 meters, Silver medal, Olympics
1972: Steeplechase, Gold medal, Olympics

Until recently, Kenyan women have had little impact on track and field. This was probably due to social pressures. Now, a generation of athletes such as Susan Sirma and Lydia Cheromei are emerging as world-class runners.

Kenyans out enjoying a day at the races.

OTHER MODERN SPORTS

Although track and field is Kenya's most successful sport, soccer remains the most popular. The national team often wins the East African Championships, and in recent years Kenya has reached the final tournament of the All African Nations Cup. However, the Kenyan team is generally not as strong as the top nations from north and west Africa.

Many soccer clubs in Kenya have strong tribal links, and this can result in fierce fights between the spectators. To try to ease this tension, the government once ordered all teams to drop their tribal names. GOR was the tribal name of one of the best known teams in Kenya. They did not wish to lose a name that was famous throughout Africa, so they re-registered as "Golf Olympic Rangers." Nobody could understand why they chose this strange title until people looked at the initials—G-O-R. Shortly afterwards, the club was given special permission to retain its old name.

In the past, tennis and golf were considered games for the white settlers, but since independence, they have become popular with rich Kenyans. Kenya stages open golf and tennis events that attract promising young players from all over the world. A few Kenyans have become good enough to play professional tennis, most notably Paul Wekessa.

Each year, Kenya is host to the Safari Rally. This is a major cross-country motor rally that is acknowledged to be one of the toughest in the world.

A car going through its paces in the Safari Rally held in Kenya each year.

The event began in 1953 as a race for local drivers to celebrate the coronation of Queen Elizabeth II. For many years, the race toured all of East Africa, but when the borders closed, it was restricted to Kenya. Professional drivers from Europe were soon attracted by the tough reputation of the race.

Today, the event has a controversial reputation, and spectators are often killed or injured when cars go out of control. Critics say that the event is no longer for Africans, and should be discontinued. However, each year, thousands of Kenyan villagers come out to enjoy the spectacle of the cars racing by.

Kenya has always had ambitions to stage major international events, and it offered to host the 1982 All African Games. Unfortunately, there were considerable problems in building the stadiums and, despite help from China, the games could not take place until 1987. These championships left Nairobi with some excellent sporting facilities, but made Kenya hesitant about trying to stage other events of this size.

FESTIVALS

PUBLIC HOLIDAYS IN KENYA are either religious occasions or anniversaries of important dates in the country's history. But not all religious holidays are celebrated throughout the country. Life in Kenya is still hard for many people, so they look forward to holidays as an opportunity to celebrate and forget their daily worries.

In nearly all traditional Kenyan societies, the most important social occasions are those that mark the passing of a group of individuals from one "age set" to another. Masai boys, at around 16, join the *moran*, or warrior group. They remain at this level for between 7 and 14 years. Later, this group is promoted to the rank of *ilterekeyani* ("il-ter-ek-e-YAHN-ee"), or recent elders. From here, they pass on to the influential "senior elder" stage, and later to "retired elders." The greatest celebration comes at the time of circumcision, which marks a boy's entrance into manhood.

Opposite: **Dancing tribal drummers.**

Below: **Young men gather, wearing skin cloaks for their *sapana* ceremony, following their ritual circumcision.**

THE NATIONAL HOLIDAYS

Holidays in Kenya bring out all the excitement and joy of the Kenyan people. In the days leading up to a holiday, overloaded buses take thousands of urban dwellers back to their villages. Most women try to purchase a new *kanga* ("KAN-gah") cloth—a colorful piece of material that wraps around the body like a skirt. There is dancing, and probably a village or family feast.

There are three main historic celebrations. Madaraka ("mah-dar-ah-kah") Day marks the anniversary of self-government. This was achieved on June 1, 1963, when Kenyans took over the running of the country prior to full independence. This is different from Uhuru ("oo-HOO-roo") Day. Celebrated on December 12, it marks the establishment of the new independent nation.

Holidays that have a historic significance are marked by parades and marches. Here, a Kikuyu group marches to celebrate Uhuru Day.

Kenyatta Day is celebrated on October 20. It marks the anniversary of Kenyatta's arrest in 1952, since his date of birth is not known.

CHRISTIAN AND MUSLIM HOLIDAYS

Christian holidays center on the church. Although the services are similar to those in the West, the atmosphere is often more colorful and noisy. There may be an African band playing, and services can run continuously, with people going outside to talk and relax, and returning to sing more hymns or listen to another sermon. The social occasion and the chance to meet people is a major part of any Kenyan church service.

For the New Year celebrations, many Kenyans get together as a family. Middle-class people may attend a dinner and dance at a big hotel. However, New Year's Day is usually a subdued celebration.

The two major Muslim holidays are Id al-Fitri and Id al-Adha. Id al-Fitri comes at the end of the month of fasting, and Id al-Adha marks the sacrificing of animals at the end of the pilgrimage. Both are celebrated by Kenya's Muslim population with feasts and special prayers in the mosque. In the coastal areas, these are more important holidays than the Christian celebrations.

The island of Lamu also stages a major celebration for Maulidi, the birthday of the Prophet Mohammed. Such celebrations take place throughout the Muslim world, but seldom with the same vigor or energy as on this Kenyan island.

The event attracts Muslim visitors from all over eastern Africa and the Indian Ocean for a week of religious ceremonies and feasting. The side attractions include dancing and ritual sword fights. Such lavish celebrations were started in the 1880s by Sheikh Habib Salih, who also founded the island's Koranic college.

Lamu Island women in their traditional Muslim dress.

OTHER SPECIAL OCCASIONS

Although not public holidays, there are several other events that are widely celebrated throughout Kenya. The Safari Rally takes place around Easter, and few people work when the cars are racing through their area. Instead, huge crowds gather at the roadside to watch this exciting spectacle.

Agriculture is central to the Kenyan economy, and so large agricultural shows are important occasions. The main events are the Nakuru Show (June), the Mombasa Show (August), and the Nairobi Show (September).

Although of less interest to the average Kenyan, the Malindi Fishing Festival is another renowned international event.

A car reaches the finish line of the Kenyan Safari Rally.

THE *KANGA*—A FESTIVAL CLOTH

During any holiday in Kenya, people will meet with friends and show off their best clothes. For many women, a holiday is a reason to buy a new *kanga*. The *kanga* is a bright rectangular cotton cloth measuring about 5 by 3 feet (1.5 by 1 meter). It can be worn in many different ways. Muslim women often wear them in pairs, one around the body, and one to cover the head and shoulders.

The first *kanga* was made in Mombasa around 1860 by sewing six very large white handkerchiefs together. Designs were hand-printed onto these in black, using a sweet potato or other vegetables as a printing block. Women wearing such distinctive cloth were referred to as *kanga*, the name for a black and white spotted guinea fowl.

As the *kanga* became popular, traders started to have them specially printed in India, and brought them to East Africa to trade. The six pieces of cloth were now replaced by one large rectangle of material, and the designs became more colorful and varied.

Although now popular all over eastern Africa, the *kanga* retains a special role in Swahili society. Swahili women may wear a *kanga* known as a *kisutu* ("ki-SOO-too") to their wedding. Young girls are presented with their first *kanga* at the beginning of puberty. The *kanga* is worn while praying as part of proper Islamic dress, and is placed over a woman's bier at her funeral.

FOOD

KENYA HAS SOME of the most fertile farmland in Africa, and the country has largely escaped the famines that have affected other regions of the continent. Common crops include wheat, potatoes, sweet potatoes, vegetables, and many types of fruit.

However, many Kenyans are very poor, and their diet is limited by income and the availability of local produce. Many people also have little concept of a healthy diet, and children who eat little except carbohydrates often develop pale, reddish hair. They can also suffer from swelling in the limbs and abdomen. Not surprisingly, Kenya has no great national dishes—the living standard of the majority of people allows for no frills, and food is generally plain but filling.

Opposite: **Bean sellers at the Karatina market.**

Left: **A typical Kenyan vegetable stall.**

Turkana girls drying fish. Some Turkana people have developed a diet based almost exclusively on fish, due to a lack of other foodstuffs in their region.

TYPICAL KENYAN FOOD

Ugali ("oo-GAL-ee") forms a major part of the diet for many Kenyans. It is inexpensive and reasonably nutritious, and many poor families depend on it to survive. It is usually made from corn ground to form a flour and then mixed with either water or milk. It is cooked until it forms a thick porridge. Sometimes it is served with vegetables or meat and dipped into gravy. It can also be rolled into a hard ball, and people often take these with them when they travel. It is also made from ground cassava or millet.

Some tribes, including the Kikuyu, prefer a diet based on beans, lentils, and corn. Villagers supplement their diet by keeping chickens, and most *shambas* (small farms) have fruit trees. Papayas, pineapples, and mangos are some of the most popular fruits. Bananas are even more important and are a major element in many people's diet. They are not only eaten raw, but are baked, steamed, fried, or roasted. Green bananas, cut into cubes, can be put into stews or soups. Boiled or steamed bananas can also be mashed into a porridge-like mixture called *matoke* ("ma-TOH-kay").

The cattle-herding tribes of the arid regions have their own special diet. The Masai, Rendille ("ren-DILL-ah"), Senguju, and many of the Samburu take most of their nourishment from a mixture of milk and animal (cattle) blood. The cattle are seldom killed, but the blood is extracted through a straw that is pushed into the animal's veins.

The Turkana have developed a method of drying milk to preserve it. They also turn some of their milk into ghee (clarified butter), or simply let it go sour. There is also a popular recipe that mixes milk with cattle blood and berries to make cakes. Unlike some of the other cattle-herding tribes, the Turkana like to eat meat in stews and soup.

In contrast, the Masai will only eat meat on special celebrations, although they will provide it for those who are sick and who need to build up their strength. The Masai also consider eating game animals as taboo, although antelopes are an exception. But many other tribes used to hunt much of their food, and some people still supplement their diet by hunting. Tribes living in the most arid areas often have to eat whatever is available. The Pokot, for example, like to hunt virtually every kind of animal, except hyena. The El Molo, although living mainly on fish, will hunt hippopotamuses, crocodiles, turtles, and birds.

The European and Asian communities have largely kept to their own traditional foods. There are many international restaurants in Nairobi and Mombasa that cater for these minority groups. There are also lively markets that supply the exotic spices required for Indian cooking.

Blood is drained from cattle to mix with milk to make a nourishing drink.

117

DRINKS

Having access to clean water is often a problem for many Kenyans. The government has provided a great number of good wells, but these can often be a long way from individual houses. It is usually the job of the women to carry heavy plastic containers of water back to the house. These are usually carried in the traditional manner, on the head or strapped onto the back. If people can afford it, they purchase water from a seller who brings a fresh supply around the village on a cart.

Two Turkana elders carrying gourds, which are used as water containers. Water in north Kenya is scarce, and so must be stored.

Tea is perhaps the most common drink in Kenya, and is usually drunk without milk. Poor people drink low grade tea, and they often add a lot of sugar to mask the taste. Coffee is becoming more popular, but is usually a social drink to be enjoyed with friends at the end of the day.

Beer is also popular, and Kenyan Breweries is the country's largest company. However, there are many traditional beers that are produced in the home. These are called *pombe* ("POM-bay"), and may be made from corn, bananas, pineapples, or millet. They are often brewed into a drink as thick as porridge. On special occasions, *pombe* is served from a single large bowl that is passed around a circle of friends.

The Masai have a traditional beer made from honey borrowed from their Dorobo neighbors. However, today the Masai beer is more likely to be brewed from sugar.

Soft drinks are bottled in Kenya and are available in all but the most remote villages. Kenya has even experimented with making an export-quality wine out of papaya.

COOKING KENYAN STYLE

Kenyans have not, like some other groups, developed cooking into an art form, but they have created a few interesting recipes that can be considered typical of Kenyan cuisine. Coconut is often used to make a distinctive and tasty sauce. The coconut is grated and soaked in water in a basket of woven grass. When the basket is squeezed, a coconut-flavored milk oozes out, while the shredded coconut remains trapped in the basket. This coconut milk may be used to cook fish, or as a sauce in which to dip *ugali*. Coconut oil is often used for cooking and adds a special rich taste to the food. It also produces a distinctive aroma.

A girl sits astride an *mbuzi* **("uhm-BOO-zee"), grating coconut to make a delicious sauce.**

Another popular sauce is made from spinach. People call this *sukuma wiki* ("soo-KOO-mah WEE-ee"), which means "finish the week," because it is cheap and used when there is not enough money to buy meat.

A RECIPE: *FUFU*

You will need 1 lb. (½ kg.) of cassava.

Peel the cassava and leave it to soak in water for four days to soften.

Cut out the central hard core. Place in a pan, cover with water, and bring to boil. Then simmer for 10 minutes.

Lift the cassava out of the saucepan and put into a mortar. Pound with a pestle until a soft dough forms.

Place the dough on a dish. *Fufu* should be served with meat or fish stew.

Enjoy your meal!

A boat crew share some typical Kenyan fare.

COOKING UTENSILS

The *mbuzi* is an important tool in Kenyan cooking. It is a small stool with a round, serrated blade fixed at one end. The cook sits astride the *mbuzi* and grates coconut on the blade. Although modern utensils are now becoming more common, many people traditionally eat their food with their hands. The meal is often taken from one large pot. The men take their food first, followed by the women, and finally the children.

As rural homes tend to be very simple, with little furniture, the family is likely to eat outdoors, probably in the shade of a tree. In fact, in some areas it would be considered extremely bad manners to eat indoors during fine weather, as this would prevent any passing friends from joining in the meal.

Cooking facilities are very primitive in the villages, and many homes still cook food over a wood fire. This continual need for firewood has become a serious environmental problem, as trees are being cut down for fuel.

Some tribes are very superstitious about how food can be prepared. For example, the Nandi live on a basic diet of milk that they believe will be magically contaminated if it comes into contact with metal. Because of this, they usually store their milk in a gourd made from a large hollowed-out fruit.

FOOD AS AN INDUSTRY

Preserving and preparing food is a major industry in Kenya. The coffee and tea industries are an important source of revenue and employ many people. Tea factories are scattered throughout the plantation area to ease transportation problems. A single factory may need two or three thousand pickers to keep it supplied.

More recently, Kenya has diversified its agriculture-linked industries. High-quality fruits are grown and canned on plantations. Great cattle herds support a leather and canned meat industry. Kenya also imports a little cocoa, and is one of the few countries in eastern Africa able to produce high-quality chocolate.

A SPECIAL TREAT

At the start of the rainy season, millions of termites leave the ground and fly off in search of new nesting sites. In towns and villages, they are often drawn toward lamps or street lights. The arrival of the termites causes great excitement, for it means a free nourishing feast. The termites are not eaten because people are hungry, but because they are considered a great delicacy. A businessman driving home in his Mercedes is just as likely to stop and gather the insects as a poor farmer. Most termites are put into a bag and taken home to be roasted. However, they are also good raw, and people will pull off the wings and chew one or two as they are collecting.

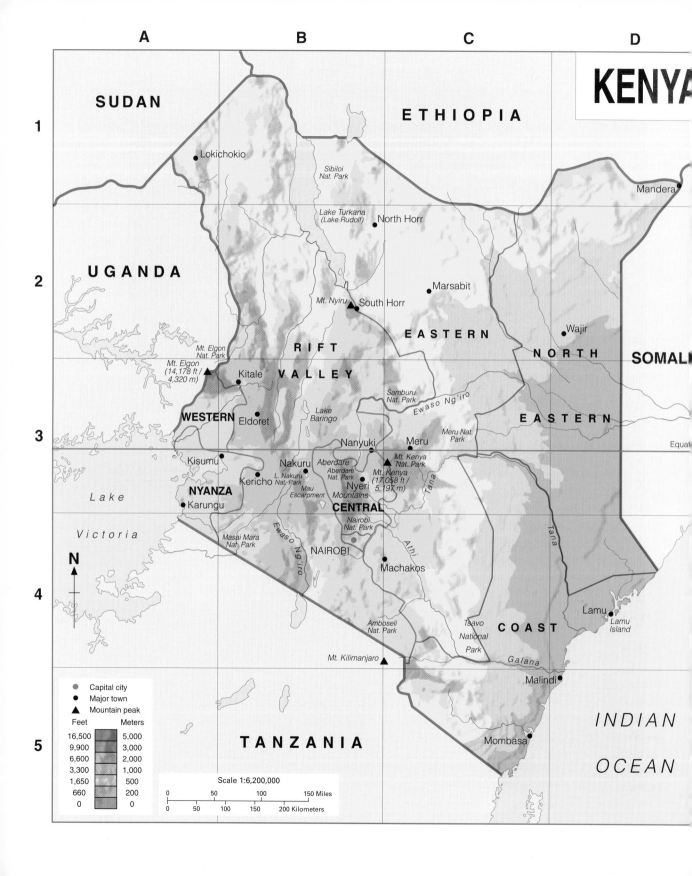

KENYA

A   **B**   **C**   **D**

1

SUDAN

ETHIOPIA

• Lokichokio

Sibiloi
Nat. Park

Mandera •

2

UGANDA

Lake Turkana
(Lake Rudolf)

North Horr •

Marsabit •

Mt. Nyiru
▲ South Horr

EASTERN

Wajir •

NORTH

SOMALI

RIFT

3

Mt. Elgon
Nat. Park

Mt. Elgon
(14,178 ft /
4,320 m) ▲

Kitale •

VALLEY

WESTERN

Eldoret •

Lake
Baringo

Samburu
Nat. Park

Ewaso Ng'iro

EASTERN

Equato

Kisumu •

Nakuru •

Nanyuki •

Meru •

Meru Nat.
Park

Aberdare
Nat. Park

Aberdare
Nat. Park

Mt. Kenya
Nat. Park

Kericho •

L. Nakuru
Nat. Park

Mt. Kenya
(17,058 ft /
5,197 m) ▲

NYANZA

Mau
Escarpment

Nyeri •

Tana

Karungu •

Mau
Mountains

Lake

CENTRAL

Nairobi
Nat. Park

4

Victoria

Masai Mara
Nat. Park

Ewaso Ng'iro

NAIROBI

Athi

N

Machakos •

Tana

Lamu •

Lamu
Island

Amboseli
Nat. Park

Tsavo
National
Park

COAST

Galana

Malindi •

5

Capital city
Major town
Mountain peak

Feet | Meters
16,500 | 5,000
9,900 | 3,000
6,600 | 2,000
3,300 | 1,000
1,650 | 500
660 | 200
0 | 0

TANZANIA

Mt. Kilimanjaro ▲

INDIAN

OCEAN

Mombasa •

Scale 1:6,200,000

0   50   100   150 Miles

0   50   100   150   200 Kilometers

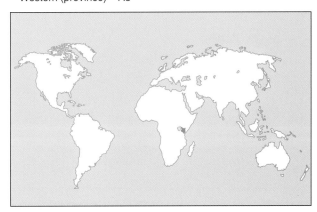

QUICK NOTES

OFFICIAL NAME
Republic of Kenya

CAPITAL
Nairobi

GOVERNMENT
KANU is the ruling party.
There are 202 seats in the National Assembly.
Elections are held every five years.

LANGUAGE
Swahili (official) and English

CURRENCY
Kenyan shilling. US$1 = about 45 shillings

POPULATION
28 million (1995 estimate), increasing by 3.3% annually

LAND AREA
224,960 square miles (582,646 sq. km)

HIGHEST MOUNTAIN
Mount Kenya (17,058 ft / 5,197 m)

MAIN TRIBES
Kikuyu (21% of population), Luo (13%), Luhya (14%), Kalenjin (11%), Kamba (11%)

LITERACY
69% of adults

INFANT MORTALITY
66 per 1000 live births

LIFE EXPECTANCY
Men: 52 years; women: 55 years

PROVINCES
Central, Rift Valley, Eastern, Nyanza, Western, North Eastern, Coast, plus the urban area of Nairobi

MAJOR RELIGIONS
Christianity, animistic tribal religions, Islam

MAJOR PUBLIC HOLIDAYS
June 1—Madaraka Day (celebrating granting of self-government)
October 20—Kenyatta Day (commemorating the arrest of Jomo Kenyatta)
December 12—Uhuru Day (Independence celebration)

MAJOR TRADING PARTNERS
United Kingdom, United States, Germany, Japan

CHIEF INCOME
Tourism, coffee, tea, cotton, oil refining.

MAJOR POLITICAL LEADERS
Jomo Kenyatta—first president of Kenya, and a symbol of Kenyan freedom in the struggle for independence; died in 1978
Ronald Ngala—leader of the opposition KADU Party, eclipsed by Kenyatta and KANU Party
Daniel arap Moi—president since 1978

GLOSSARY

Bajuni ("ba-JOON-i")
A Bantu tribe of Kenya.

Bantu ("BAN-too")
Describes African tribes speaking a common language, Bantu.

baobab ("BAY-oh-bab")
African tree with a thick trunk that stores water.

bwana ("BWAH-nah")
Short for *baba wa wana*, meaning "the father of many sons," a traditional way to address men.

Cushitic ("koo-SHIT-ik")
A family of African languages.

El Molo ("el MO-lo")
A primitive Cushitic tribe of Kenya.

harambee ("hah-rahm-BAY")
Swahili word that means "pull together."

jambo ("JAM-boh")
Kiswahili for "hello."

kanga ("KAN-gah")
Colorful cloth worn wrapped around the body like a skirt.

karibuni ("kar-i-BOON-ee")
Kiswahili for "welcome."

Kigogo ("ki-GO-go")
A game of Arab origin played in east Africa.

Kikuyu ("ki-KOO-yoo")
A group of African people originally from the area of Mount Kenya.

Kipsigis ("KIP-si-gis")
A Nilotic tribe of west Kenya.

Kiswahili ("ki-swah-HEE-lee")
Bantu language and national language of Kenya.

laibon ("LAI-bon")
A Masai fortune-teller.

Masai ("mah-SAI")
A Nilotic tribe of cattle raisers of north Kenya.

matoke ("ma-TOH-kay")
A dish made fom cooked bananas.

mbira ("m-BIR-ah")
String musical instrument.

mbuzi ("m-BOO-zee")
An instrument used for grating or grinding food.

Moran ("MAHR-en")
A rank of development for young Masai men.

ngoma ("n-GO-mah")
Large drums played in traditional Kenyan music.

Nilotic ("ni-LOT-ik")
Language or people from the area of the Nile.

obukano ("o-boo-KAHN-o")
String musical instrument.

pombe ("POM-bay")
Traditional Kenyan beer made from corn, bananas, pineapple, or millet.

Samburu ("sahm-BOO-roo")
Nilotic tribe of Kenya.

ugali ("oo-GAL-ee")
Staple food of east Africa, made from grains.

Wasimba ("wah-SIM-bah")
Legendary tribe of Kenya thought to have helped drive out the Portguese.

BIBLIOGRAPHY

Adamson, Joy. *Born Free: A Lioness of Two Worlds.* New York: Pantheon, 1987.

Azevedo, Mario, editor. *Kenya: The Land, the People & the Nation.* Durham, North Carolina: Carolina Academic Press, 1993.

Burch, Joann J. *Kenya: Africa's Tamed Wilderness.* New York: Macmillan Children's Book Group, 1992.

Houston, Dick. *Safari Adventure.* New York: Cobblehill, 1991.

Maren, Michael. *The Land & People of Kenya.* New York: Harper Collins Children's Books, 1989.

Ng'Weno, Fleur. *Kenya.* North Pomfret, Vermont: Trafalgar, 1992.

INDEX

INDEX

INDEX

DATE			